I0455336

Lessons Learned

How Acceptance, Vulnerability,
Forgiveness, and Compassion Make Sense to Me

ROBERT ACKERMAN

WITH

J. IBEH AGBANYIM

LESSONS LEARNED
HOW ACCEPTANCE, VULNERABILITY, FORGIVENESS, AND COMPASSION MAKE SENSE TO ME

Copyright © 2019 Robert Ackerman with J. Ibeh Agbanyim.

All rights reserved. No part of this book may be used or reproduced by any means, graphic, electronic, or mechanical, including photocopying, recording, taping or by any information storage retrieval system without the written permission of the author except in the case of brief quotations embodied in critical articles and reviews.

The views expressed in this work are solely those of the author and do not necessarily reflect the views of the publisher, and the publisher hereby disclaims any responsibility for them.

iUniverse books may be ordered through booksellers or by contacting:

iUniverse
1663 Liberty Drive
Bloomington, IN 47403
www.iuniverse.com
1-800-Authors (1-800-288-4677)

Because of the dynamic nature of the Internet, any web addresses or links contained in this book may have changed since publication and may no longer be valid. The views expressed in this work are solely those of the author and do not necessarily reflect the views of the publisher, and the publisher hereby disclaims any responsibility for them.

Any people depicted in stock imagery provided by Getty Images are models, and such images are being used for illustrative purposes only. Certain stock imagery © Getty Images.

ISBN: 978-1-5320-8541-3 (sc)
ISBN: 978-1-5320-8543-7 (hc)
ISBN: 978-1-5320-8542-0 (e)

Library of Congress Control Number: 2019917814

Print information available on the last page.

iUniverse rev. date: 11/05/2019

Contents

Part IV Compassion

Acknowledgments

*E*xpressing myself in writing is more difficult than I ever could have imagined. It is humbling and yet rewarding, and without the constant support and encouragement of family, friends, and colleagues, it would be almost impossible. I want to thank everyone who has ever offered a positive comment and took the time to coach and teach me. They cared, and it mattered.

Through my active participation in the world around me, I have learned to always be humbled by and grateful for my unique place in it. I see and feel the rewards as well as the fulfillment in helping others achieve their dreams, and this is first and foremost in my mind as I move forward each day.

Once again, a special thanks to Ibeh, who helped guide and encourage me to once again put my thoughts into words.

Author's Note

I love stories, and I have collected a few over the course
of my life and career that resonate with me. I've worked
in both the public and private sectors. I've also wandered into
others as life may have it. Each chapter here intends to tell a
story to humanize the topic without offering a concrete solution;
instead I let readers draw their own conclusions and hopefully
find the story useful.

Part I shares how accepting people the way they are—
especially after learning about them and their past—has been
one of my biggest challenges to overcome. Sometimes I tend
to dwell on people's past mistakes rather than accept their new
attitudes. Intellectually, I know that all people learn and grow.
I hope that sharing my stories and learning how I am working
through this personal issue will encourage others to examine
their acceptance challenges.

Part II is about how I have noticed over the years the enormous
power that comes from being vulnerable to experiences that
were usually not easily discussed. I have learned that sharing
those experiences from a place of vulnerability provides much
relief and even transformation.

Part III is about forgiveness. I have realized that forgiveness
isn't for the perpetrator but is rather for the offended, and this

has lessened the psychological weight I carry each time I feel hurt by others.

Part IV is about compassion. Having compassion toward others has shaped the way I see others and myself. I have been on the other side of compassion, when I was met with aloofness, resentment, and insensitivity. It's painful and discomfiting to be on the receiving side of a lack of compassion.

There is no prescribed sequence to follow when reading this book, as each part stands on its own. The truth is that we all have individual life lessons and stories. I present mine to liberate myself from the burden of carrying them alone as well as offer new perspectives to my readers.

With that said, even though these are my stories and experiences, they might not work for everyone.

Part I

Acceptance

1

Dream Big

A clash always exists between reality and illusion. Reality is what is known from an observer's position and is generally accepted over a period of time. On the other hand, others can narrowly accept illusion, even though it's real to the person who's experiencing it. In this instance, attention to what is at stake can be overlooked. Having a clear understanding of a particular situation is a critical component in a relationship. This means focusing on the challenge at hand and not being distracted by different previous experiences, especially when the new situation requires a different set of approaches in problem solving. In this case, it would be wise to look at the situation from both your and the other person's perspective. That is, have a 360-degree view before you make a decision, and then engage in an honest discussion with the person involved in the process to ensure that your own blind spots are not clouding you.

My aha moment occurred when I understood that other people's experiences and how they interpreted them differently than I did wasn't about them; rather, it was about me discovering myself through those experiences. In hindsight, many similar events had happened in my life in different areas, such as leadership, relationships, and spirituality, to mention a few, in which I missed the opportunity to ask different questions. This new insight led me to understand that the more I think about how I experience my daily events, the more I realize that how I focus my attention on my experiences determines my response or reaction to those events. I have also realized that those things I focus less attention on start to diminish.

For instance, when I initially decided to resign from my comfortable job to pursue my passion, it was challenging to my family and me because it was a new frontier. But as I continued to pursue my passion, my fears and worries about missing my previous comfortable job started to become less important to me. I sometimes feel that it's good every now and then to have my head in the clouds because if I look the second time, what was once an unrealistic idea could begin to make sense to me.

As I mentioned earlier, it was frightening and unsettling the first time I thought about leaving my comfortable job to pursue a different passion. It was entirely different from my familiar situation, especially the thought of potentially losing everything. Initially it felt unreal, but when I acted on it, a whole new world opened for my family, others, and me. So it is human to have our heads in the clouds every now and then. Our quest to imagine the impossible becomes possible through verbalizing and acting on it. And sometimes suppressing that very feeling delays our destiny.

When I think about everything that has ever been created, designed, or actualized, they have come through realized ideas and imagination, never a place of the familiar and routine. Rather it's from a place of uncertainty. It makes sense to accept the unfamiliar and different. We should embrace unfamiliarity as new information, and hopefully we will make a discovery in the process of entertaining the unfamiliar. Another way to look at the unfamiliar is to be aware of the possibility of learning while sitting in this unfamiliar territory. Learning is difficult without initially positioning our minds to accept the possibility of doing so.

Psychologist Susan David talks about emotional agility as a way to emphasize the importance of allowing ourselves to be emotionally agile in the midst of emotional crossroads, and how we explain our emotional state determines if we'll be emotionally rigid or agile. It would be difficult to have our heads in the clouds if we constantly want to validate only our acceptable emotions and repress natural, negative ones, such as sadness, denial, and so on. It's known that rigid denial does not work and that suppressing an emotion amplifies the very sentiment we're trying to subdue. This seems to suggest that discomfort is a required condition of life and our emotions are data. Our emotions tell us how we're doing and where we are in terms of weaknesses, strengths, resiliency, regrets, and what we care about. Ignoring our emotions without examining them amplifies the very ones we try to avoid.

I have learned that any emotions or situations I try to avoid never go away, especially in relationships, whether business or personal. How I respond to relationships is a reflection of my internal well-being. The sooner I recognize the situation and find a practical way to solve it, the quicker I don't have to emotionally compartmentalize it. It's impossible to remain serious twenty-four seven in life. In other words, sometimes it's healthy to leave the office and go for a walk or do any physical activity to create a balanced life because life is an adventure. Enjoy the ride. All failures are learning experiences. I'm certain that life puts walls in front of us to see how badly we want something, not to stop us. I can think of three simple ways I can balance my life.

1. After a long day of challenging decision-making and ensuring that deadlines are met and clients and employees are happy, it's fitting to shift gears once we pull into the garage and spend time reflecting and reenergizing. People obviously feed off our energy. In other words, if I return home from work with stress filled energy, my wife and children can sense it right at the door, which could change the atmosphere in the house. It's always a good idea after a warm reception from your family to politely ask them to give you some time to relax alone, take your shoes off, put your feet up, and take deep breaths for at least fifteen to thirty minutes. This shift helps reset and settle our bodies and minds. When we repeat this exercise regularly, it becomes a habit and a way of life.

2. Asking for help takes courage. It is a sign of strength, not weakness. It takes courage to admit what we do not know and seek assistance or direction. When we lack knowledge of how to do something, it can be frustrating. But if we can pause and understand that not knowing something can be a catalyst to seek knowledge, then we can start to seek information through available means, such as asking for people who have knowledge in that particular area, googling the information and reading materials from credible sources, and reaching out to people who have experienced it. The worst thing to do when we are stuck and don't know what to do is to feel helpless and hopeless. These feelings may not serve us well; rather, they escalate our frustrations and can distort our sense of reasoning regarding that particular issue. Not knowing where we stand is inhumane because we will start to do a disservice to ourselves and others who could have benefited from us, if we had obtained the necessary knowledge. It is a disservice

to humanity because we purposely decided not to ask for or seek out more information. And once we are resolved to not knowing, we have essentially denied ourselves the opportunity to improve our capacity to learn. I'm certain that there is strength in asking for help. By asking for help, we gain knowledge, and when knowledge is translated into results, change happens.

3. Learning not to win every discussion has made me a better person. It can be tempting to want to be right all the time, especially in the boardroom or in relationships. The best lesson I have learned in life is to allow others to be themselves and express how they really feel without worrying about me judging them. I have noticed that when I'm free to express myself unhindered, I tend to unconsciously reciprocate and extend the same courtesy to others. I'm also less likely to take myself too seriously. Empowering others to be authentic validates my authentic self. Conversely, wanting to win every argument makes me emotionally rigid.

These three simple ways of balancing my life have helped me tremendously. They have allowed me to accept things I cannot change and make every effort to change the things I can. They have allowed me to not take myself too seriously because life is interesting when I can make fun of myself. That way, when others make fun of me, it doesn't diminish my self-esteem. These simple lessons remind me to keep imagining the unimaginable, for in the midst of my imagination lies the great opportunity to live a meaningful life. Having our heads in the clouds represents a glimpse of humanity that reminds us we'll never know it all.

For example, consider Dr. Eben Alexander, a terrific Harvard-trained neurosurgeon who believes deeply in science and, like other scientists, argued at one time that there is no such thing as a near-death experience. Then he had an afterlife experience that changed his entire worldview. He chronicled his experience in his best-selling book, *Proof of Heaven*. Today, Dr. Alexander travels around the world speaking about his afterlife experience.

Evidently, no matter how intelligent we think we are, we'll never know it all. This intellectual humility keeps me humble and hungry to know more. Merely understanding this concept in itself is awareness. The quest to know that experiences of any sort and by all measures are lessons that force us closer to our humanity makes us human. Therefore, this very thought suggested to me that our heads will sometimes be in the clouds, and we should be at peace with that.

Reality and illusion always coexist, and we need both of them to make a difference. Others are more likely to accept reality rather than an illusion because it might have been tested over and over again. On the other hand, an illusion doesn't exist to a larger extent because not many people have attempted it. Inventions are results of a practicalized illusion. But having a clear understanding of a particular situation is a critical component in a relationship, and accepting the fact that there are always more than two sides to every story gives us room for other possibilities. Knowing that fear of failure is a compelling force for discovery can be a pathway to achieving big goals, for in our failures come our collective experiences, which in turn could result in our shared humanity.

2

The Importance of Having a Twenty-Five-Year Plan

*I*f I were to ask my thirteen-year-old self to develop a twenty-five-year plan, that adolescent would probably have a good laugh. At that age, I barely knew myself, let alone how to devise a quarter-century plan. However, as I grew older, I became increasingly aware of the importance of having a short- and a long-term plan.

Fast-forward to my twenties, the time when I started to question certain things in life, such as, "Why am I here? Where am I going? What is my purpose in life?" Although these were mere questions without any tangible answers in sight, the more I thought about those inquiries, the more I found reason to ask additional queries. Over the years, asking questions motivated me to believe in the importance of a twenty-five-year plan.

There are several reasons why I have a twenty-five-year plan, especially now. And by the word *now*, I mean in the sense of the present moment or constant change. What I think I might be perceiving at one point in time often changes to something else entirely based on how I perceive it in the present moment.

In other words, there's no such thing as now, only the

way I once knew something compared with the way in which I perceive it in the present, making good use of what I have learned along the way. For example, during my teenage years, if I claimed that I knew how to remain in good physical health, I would only be claiming such a thing based on memories of what I had heard, read, and possibly seen. The idea of physical health is based on the repetition of what I have exposed myself to in terms of physical health.

From reading scientific journals and watching physical fitness exercises, I have come to realize how important exercise is to my physical well-being. However, in order to be in good physical health, it's important to put into action what I have read and witnessed others demonstrate. Simply reading physical exercise–related materials or watching others work out can never make me physically healthy. It's only when I put what I know into action that my physical health is affected. In a few words, being in good physical health means staying alive.

Staying alive is the most important part of my twenty-five-year plan. While it's impossible to be immune from the risks and dangers of life, making a conscious decision to do things that will not jeopardize my life designates the important task of remaining alive a top priority. It's said, "Life is 10 percent what happens to you and 90 percent how you react to it."

It's not what happens to us that matters. Rather, it is our opinions about what happens to us matter. So being alive has everything to do with how we see our world. In this sense, being alive is not about breathing in air and exhaling. Rather, our perception about our world determines the quality of the life we live. Perception in this sense has everything to do with our twenty-five-year plan. So, where does perception come from, and how does it connect to our quarter-century plan?

Perception comes from a collection of memories. We

formulate views about a particular event based on a series of events and life exposures. Traumatic exposures can have a damaging effect on the way we perceive our world. The same principles apply when we are exposed to a loving and stable childhood. It tends to inform how we negotiate life's challenges.

So, our twenty-five-year plan should include the ability to question our perspectives and remain open to being vulnerable when necessary to learn new ways of seeing old stories. When we allow ourselves to interrogate our internal, private hell, we begin to liberate our minds, moving from rigidity to agility. Since our memories shape our perceptions about the world we live in, it would make sense to have a mantra. A mantra, by definition, "a word or phrase that is often repeated and expresses a particular strong belief."

Most people have a mantra that helps them get through situations in life. Some call them "mantra-affirmation words." The phrase can motivate a person to persevere or project positive energy. In corporate America, for example, UPS's old slogan was, "What can brown do for you?" For many years, UPS was known by this slogan, until recently, when it was changed to "We [heart] logistics."

So, when people are on course for something greater, they tend to invoke a phrase that energizes them to keep moving. That's why it's important to have a mantra that motivates us to stay on course. It could be any inspiring phrase that can energize individuals to reach for a higher goal. In this twenty-five-year-plan journey, we need two things: a mantra that keeps us on track as a reminder of our commitment and a cognitive attitude that can keep us engaged to stay on course. Today, my mantra is, live a passion filled life.

Our mental health plays a critical role in keeping us connected to our twenty-five-year plan. The old saying, "garbage in, garbage out," has a profound impact on the actual information we feed our minds. Our minds can only deliver the information we put into them and maintain. The mind does not discriminate. That is, our minds have no other colors besides human hues. The mind performs best based on what the owner programs into it. If the mind is corrupt, it will only attract like-minded people and ideas.

So, what is it about the mind that can shape our twenty-five-year plan? An unstable mind produces unstable results; it is proud about it because that is all it knows how to do. If we embark on a quarter-century plan, it will guide us to investigate what our minds are producing and the benefits of these results.

At this point in my life and looking back in my life's rearview mirror, I can agree that the human mind is capable of adapting to new information. As I have grown in knowledge and truth, I have begun to understand, for example, why I took chances in moving from one stable company to a start-up and how I was energized to accept the challenges that came with this new organization. The mind knows what our intellect often does not want us to know. Also, we blossom when we allow our minds to tell us what our intellect cannot, and when our heads, lips, and actions align in harmony, we start to do things differently.

Our twenty-five-year plan will guide us to the realization that "the unexamined life is not worth living." Having this plan requires reassessing and renegotiating what we claim to know and allowing ourselves to challenge our blind spots, those things that we cannot see because we are so focused on the familiar and are unwilling to accept these challenges. Our blind spots may also be those things we're unaware of. Sometimes our body language speaks volumes more than we can imagine. According to Joe Navarro, a retired FBI special agent who served for twenty-five years and specialized in interrogating spies and dangerous criminals, the average person blinks sixteen to twenty times per minute. Blinking increases when we are under stress, someone questions us aggressively, and so forth. These gestures could become our blind spots if we lack the knowledge about them. But if we take some time to understand one another, we could learn how to create psychological comfort with people and avoid creating unnecessary discomfort for others.

A twenty-five-year plan can include taking time to understand human dynamics from a place of caring and compassion rather than one of distrust and fear. It's always telling when we can take our time to relate to people who under normal circumstances may not have access to us. Such a gesture reveals a lot about our caring spirits. And *spirit*, in this context, is not used in the sense of religion or religiosity but rather that of connecting with something outside of ourselves.

Spiritual intelligence is incorporated in my twenty-five-year plan. The ability to recognize that we are entitled to connect to something or someone outside of ourselves represents one step into a new dimension. To be in harmony, one has to believe in something. Even those who claim not to believe in anything believe in not believing, which is a belief in itself. The ability to respect those who have beliefs different from our own is one step in the right direction.

Belief is essentially an art of humanity. If we have faith in humanity, we are fundamentally practicing our belief. By making a conscious effort to recognize that we're supposed to connect to self, something, a place, or someone is a demonstration of belief in itself. When we make a conscious effort to have a twenty-five-year plan and intentionally adhere to it, the chances of living a fulfilled life are higher than when we don't have any plan at all.

A twenty-five-year plan is a road map that leads us to our destination, seemingly suggesting that in order to have a road map, we must first have a plan or clear idea of where we want to go or what we'd like to do. The map simply validates how to get to the destination and what we require for it. That is, a traveler has to have a destination in mind before he or she starts on a journey.

If a traveler doesn't clearly know where he or she is going, at least the individual has an idea of what the area has to offer. That in itself is the beginning of a plan. In other words, big plans begin with an idea or a thought. To have an idea is to have a plan. An idea can motivate someone to start a plan. To have an idea and a plan is to have a focus because success never occurs by accident. So, for a traveler to arrive at his or her destination, this person must have a road map and a high level of focus or concentration.

Having a map doesn't guarantee a safe arrival. It's almost guaranteed that obstacles will arise along the way, such as roadblocks, heavy traffic, mechanical issues with travel equipment, a traveler who becomes sick or loses courage, and so on. What makes the journey successful is that, despite all these obstacles, the traveler keeps pushing and persevering. If a break becomes necessary, he or she might take one and then keep going without minding the naysayers.

Naysayers will try to discourage us along the way, but we should not give too much attention or energy to them because they can sometimes kill our dreams. Instead, we can view their distractions as a motivating force to reach our destiny. If we succumb to our naysayers' pressures, they may simply suggest that the journey was never clear in our minds and in print in the first place. When an idea is first developed in the laboratory of our minds, we meditate on it and then put it in writing. It makes the notion much more practical and attainable than when it's just an idea without wheels.

A friend taught me this powerful lesson about setting and reaching goals. He shared with me how he got his wife and child involved in creating vision boards. Each individual's board features an itemized project to be accomplished within the next six months. Additionally, each person will explain to the group how he or she intends to achieve these set goals. Every time a project is completed, the individual checks it off on the board and moves to the next one until every single item is achieved.

At the end of the sixth month, the whole family convenes and reviews their individual vision boards. At this point, any incomplete projects might be carried over to the next six-month period, if possible. After reviewing individual projects on the vision board, everyone creates a new set for the next six months. This simple but effective practice is repeated over and over again with renewed plans as each is accomplished.

There's power in creating vision boards and staying focused on accomplishing the objectives that we set for ourselves. An organized, step-by-step approach to accomplish a goal is tied to the twenty-five-year plan, which represents a practical mental picture of where we're going. It's very difficult to accomplish what we have never imagined. Thoughts precede action; action brings about change or results.

Better put, a twenty-five-year plan has no relevance if it's not lived. A plan only makes sense when we set it in motion by moving toward its realization and translating it into evidence. Evidently, being alive indicates that there's work yet to be done, and a process can help guide us to accomplish the work, which might require us to come up with a mantra or affirmation that can inspire us to stay energized, physically fit, mentally disciplined, and in strong spiritual health.

The idea of having a twenty-five-year plan might seem ambiguous, but the hardest part is getting started. Considering the plan from a position of a one-day-at-a-time approach can motivate us to begin because the worst thing to do is not start at all. I believe that everything worth doing is worth doing well. And doing it well entails having a plan. Once we create a mental map in the theater of our minds and commit in practice how to go about it, achieving such goals becomes a real and awaiting adventure.

3

How Can I Accept This?

I have experienced certain situations throughout my adult life that led me to ask in the silence of my heart, *How can I accept this?* Looking back in my life's rearview mirror, I recognized that those past challenges prepared me to become who I am today, including the humble successes I have encountered along the way. Success can be intimidating and overwhelming, just as failures can fuel our progress in any setting of our lives. The biggest obstacle is that sometimes we cannot predict when and how those challenging moments will start or end. However, it sure feels good to know that life challenges are inevitable and they will confront us whether we're ready or not. But I recognize now that I must first see the challenges clearly in order to ask the right questions during challenging times so I at least have some point of reference for how to entertain such events. I am also aware that I sometimes face situations I have no prior experience in solving. But I have built resilience and tolerance over the years as I have attempted to solve hundreds of life challenges, large and small.

Research has documented that about 90 percent of us will experience at least one serious traumatic event during our lives (Southwick and Charney 2012). That means nine out of ten of us will experience a traumatic event in our lifetimes. This statistic makes it absolutely important to know that we'll need resilience to weather life's storms. Interestingly, no two persons will respond to an identical traumatic event in precisely the same way. We will not know how we respond to trauma until it happens. We can read all the literature in the world on how to handle them, but until we have personally encountered one, we'll never grasp its weight or how to fittingly respond to it.

So, I have accepted the hard truth that the vast majority of us will experience traumatic events in our lifetimes. I know I've had my fair share of life experiences. Comprehending this hard truth can at least allow us to acknowledge life's complexities and what it means to be human. In other words, whether we're rich or poor, religious or nonreligious, or smart or dumb, we all have one thing in common, the universal nature of human suffering.

Going through bitter experiences has, in some ways, brought the best out of me. One experience was when I lost my father. I still choke up whenever I'm alone and thinking about him. My father, a high school dropout who worked all hours to provide for his family, was my hero. I can still hear his voice encouraging me to never be afraid to push beyond my frontier of incompetence. By exposing myself to new challenges, I will learn, grow in knowledge, and build resilience. I never truly appreciated his life experiences until late in my life. His death opened me to be vulnerable and be in touch with my emotional self. I began to build resilience around death after experiencing the passing of loved ones and friends.

A good analogy is exercising, weight lifting, running, and so on. It's impossible to be in good shape just by watching somebody else lift weights or jog. We can observe other people working out all day long, but until we get in the arena and exercise, watching them will never make us look or feel fit. Similarly, we build resilience by entering the arena of life and experiencing it.

Child-rearing is another good example of resilience. As a father, I only built resilience in child-rearing after my own children were born. In other words, resilience in child-rearing can only occur when we place ourselves in proximity to the very group we want to build resilience for. We develop tolerance in the process of building resilience.

The science of acceptance has been identified as an ingredient in the ability to tolerate highly stressful situations among survivors of extreme environmental hardship and life threats. Acceptance and tolerance go hand in hand because we must have experienced acceptance in order to tolerate a situation or person. I clearly had to accept the situation as it was, not as it could have been, so I could tolerate how I felt about the loss of my father. I came to terms with that loss; thus, I became able to function again in the affairs of life when I made this mental leap.

On another note, everything we do, whether in relationships, social experiences, or the workplace, obviously has this duality of purpose (acceptance and tolerance). In the workplace, we have little power to choose our coworkers. An organizational structure dictates how management delegates job tasks according to experience, skills, and the order of work needs, so the chances of working with a coworker we don't like are higher. In this instance, individuals must initially accept the truth that sometimes we may work with people we don't necessarily like to socialize with, but for the purpose of work, we tend to tolerate them within the work space.

My experience in the workplace with a healthy atmosphere is that we must sometimes practice acceptance in order to tolerate our colleagues; however, if the workplace becomes hostile and toxic, then it becomes a concern. Tolerance is learned and a hallmark of working with one another in any capacity, but we must first accept a situation before tolerating whatever comes from it.

We lack tolerance when we reject acceptance. In fact, we cannot practice civility without acceptance and tolerance of one another. Negotiation emerges from acceptance and tolerance. In any attempt to negotiate a business deal, a piece of legislature, or a relational issue, we must yield to resilience, acceptance, and tolerance. Without these virtues, it would be difficult to coexist and civilly engage in any discourse. So it is reasonable on the subconscious and conscious levels to constantly evaluate how accepting and tolerating we are as individuals, a community, and a nation. Asking this simple but critical question—How can I accept this?—can resolve the majority of humanity's problems because it exposes the state of our minds and intentions. That's because "how" usually requires steps and processes.

I gain an opportunity to explore other options and possibilities when I start my question with "How?" This also allows me to "get in the balcony"—that is, to step back and examine the situation holistically. During that process, I may discover things I once overlooked or overanalyzed. In an attempt to do the work, I accept the situation and start to design possible answers by consulting with others who are more knowledgeable in my areas of struggle. The initial work starts by confronting the truth or reality. We accept life's realities by admitting our inadequacies or limitations in omniscience (accepting that we don't know everything).

In my quest to understand what acceptance means to me, I began paying particular attention to how people interact with one another in groups or one on one and how individuals used the word *acceptance*. I next looked into literature in which events expose people who are reevaluating their lives and situations.

In this instance, I came across a story of the physicist Alfred Nobel, who was known for inventing dynamite and detonators, a powerful and deadly explosive apparatus that could destroy lives but demolish old buildings and start new construction. He owned 355 patents when he died in 1896.

Before his death, he had a new experience that changed his life. Alfred's brother, Ludvig, died of heart attack in France. In a case of mistaken identity, a French reporter wrote the obituary as if Alfred Nobel had passed. In the obituary, the reporter remembered Alfred as a "merchant of death" who became wealthy from developing new ways to "mutilate and kill."

Although the error was corrected, Alfred had unfortunately already read his own obituary, which must have profoundly affected him in such a manner that he decided to will his wealth to charity. And thus, that was how he started the Nobel prizes for outstanding people in the fields of physics, chemistry, physiology, medicine, and literature. That incorrect obituary motivated Alfred to change his course, and he recognized the need to rewrite his history and how others would remember him.

When I read Alfred Nobel's story, I realized how important it is to be introspective and envision how I want to be remembered—that is, the kind of legacy I want to leave. I considered living a full life to incorporate accepting the mind shift that I have made because of real-life experience and reading. As Peter McWilliams rightly said, "The bottom-line question: Do we pursue what we want, or do we do what's comfortable?" (Hinds 2016).

I have realized and accepted the hard fact that living a fulfilled life requires me to accept discomfort as a part of life growth, for there is no growth without discomfort. We feel vulnerable and lost in our discomforts, but as we push through them, we discover our new beginnings.

It is important to note that, in order to accept something, we must first seek to understand it, which can put us in close proximity and lead us to building resiliency in life. And once we build resiliency, acceptance then opens the door to tolerance. Occasionally it is good to step aside and examine the legacy we are leaving to ensure it is the kind we wish to bequeath.

Part II
Vulnerability

4

An Attractive Feature

*V*ulnerability work is a journey, never a destination. Though it can be uncomfortable, unpredictable, and frightening, it is simultaneously attractive. We must face discomfort so we can grow in any area of life. Before I started my vulnerability work, I used to do whatever it took to avoid the pain that susceptibility may bring. Discomfort from vulnerability is inevitable, but I had to sit with my pain long enough to learn and grow from it. Eventually I realized that the more I practiced vulnerability, the clearer it became how little I knew about it. The more I learned about vulnerability, the more I began to feel like I was living in a fish tank where everybody was watching. It was necessary to accept this feeling so I could begin being comfortable in my skin.

I have noticed over the years that while my vulnerability work has scared some people out of my life, it has attracted others, strengthening our friendships. Even the idea of writing this book was a demonstration of my work on vulnerability. I remember the first time I met Julio Ibeh Agbanyim, who helped me write this book. We met at my office while he was working as a driver for a package delivery business.

As days went by and our discussions began to expand

beyond package deliveries, I began to see his potential and many talents. I learned he had degrees in business and psychology, and he was working on his PhD in industrial-organization psychology. It blew my mind to learn that he had acquired these degrees while working as a delivery driver, which increased my curiosity about his commitments as both as a graduate and a deliveryman.

One day, Ibeh brought a manuscript for me to review and, if possible, comment on the content. I was surprised to learn that he had written the text, and I was deeply impressed when I read it. It was about how to find balance in work and life by engaging our minds and outwardly demonstrating this engagement. I found the topic so captivating and intriguing that I was moved to endorse this work, which later became the first of his many published books.

Now he was not only my delivery driver and a multiple-degree holder, he was also a published author. After his book was published, he told me he planned to go on a book tour to speak about his work. I asked when he had time to do all these things, delivering packages for ten hours a day, five days a week, while also writing and publishing a book and now going on a book tour.

Through Ibeh's work and dedication, we bonded and became friends. Meeting Ibeh from a place of vulnerability allowed me to connect with him and brought us closer to the work that we now do together. I developed this trust with Ibeh through the way he carries himself and his ability to share his vulnerable moments, his willingness to serve others, and his caring and meaningful conversations with his customers. This manuscript is the second work we have collaborated on, with many more to follow.

I believe that vulnerability is attractive because it has

the potential to bring human beings with good intentions together for a greater purpose. Most importantly, when we do vulnerability work the right way, it breeds healing and amplifies our humanity. Ibeh and I remain good friends because of qualities we share, including our openness to life.

Doing vulnerability work has led me to ponder a few reasons why people are hesitant to be vulnerable. Over the years, I have uncovered several motivating factors within myself that have hindered my vulnerability work.

I primarily believe that people do not like to be vulnerable because they do not know how it will turn out when they honestly confide in loved ones. I still carry this fear of how people will react to my openness about my truth, but I still choose to be open with people who deserve my openness. I also see a self-earnestness associated with pushing through my fears.

To others who are still trying to understand why they have difficulty being open with their loved ones, I have one message: "You are not alone." It is a never-ending work. I find myself experiencing it every day. I am certain that the benefits outweigh the risks. One of the benefits is to be at peace with oneself without carrying the weight of feeling rejected.

The fear of being rejected is another reason why it is difficult to be vulnerable. When you open yourself up to someone, you cannot know for sure that they will not reject or avoid you because of the new information they have learned about you. Thus, one of the ways to counteract my fear is to confront it. For example, some people dread stage fright or feel it is nerve-racking, but most individuals overcome it by getting some lessons and standing on stage to speak. Such internal behavior or self-talk helps me to have compassion for people who have made mistakes, regardless how severe.

My previous experience with people who honestly confided

in me and how that openness made me feel can keep me from being open about my own challenges. If I were not accepting of others' openness in the past, I might project a similar reaction onto others when I wish to be open with them. In other words, if I have judged others in the past, I might expect others to judge me.

This cognitive script I wrote about myself bothered me for many years. Yet I was able to overcome those feelings of unhealthy projection by examining how I feel whenever I am confronted by a situation that would place me in a position of judging others. I'm also aware that calling myself out whenever I feel like judging others helps me to rewrite my cognitive scripts.

Lack of trust in oneself and low self-esteem can lead people to be rigid. When we see ourselves from a negative perspective, we tend to self-preserve by overcompensating for our emotions. I notice that whenever I start to feel vulnerable in a particular area of my life, it is because I am second-guessing myself in that specific zone, especially when it has to do with constructive risk-taking. But I have realized over the years that people perceive us the way we see ourselves. The way we carry ourselves in public and private speaks volumes about who we are.

Once our self-image is compromised, we are drastically disadvantaged in our vulnerability work. I am aware that whenever I'm grappling with some personal challenges, my thought process always comes back to how I view myself in those situations. Sometimes I tend to exaggerate a challenge, and if I do not check this tendency, it could result in an overreaction. I have also learned that the more I trust myself, the more confident and vulnerable I become to people who deserve my vulnerability and, most importantly, the more I know myself.

It is amazing how people can sense when others are rigid and do not display self-confidence. I'm convinced that both vulnerability and rigidity have presence. By interacting with some people who were not vulnerable, I began questioning how vulnerable I was. Being open to others carries certain attractive features. When we are vulnerable, people like being around us and open with us, and they even look out for us. Vulnerability carries these features because of its presence.

Vulnerability speaks a different language and has a code. Its language says, "I care to hear what you have to say." Its code says, "I'm human, and it's okay to be human." Once we understand that vulnerability has presence, we begin to live a full life because invulnerability causes us to carry the world on our shoulders. It is heavy, ugly, resentful, limiting, and deceiving.

I have lived in both worlds. It is never easy to carry a weight alone. We can share our concerns with thousands of well-meaning and caring people in the world. Vulnerability is all about accepting who we are and doing something with the person we are. Invulnerability is about knowing ourselves from a distorted view and wanting to protect and hide our inadequacies.

Our distorted views about ourselves may come from our childhood experiences of abuse and neglect, dysfunction in our marriages or relationships, or workplace or schoolyard bullying. These are possible platforms where we mostly pick up distorted views about ourselves. Somehow, we convince ourselves that covering up those unhealed psychological wounds will be of great benefit to us. Unfortunately, that's not necessarily the case. As we expose our inadequacies and embrace our authenticities, we instead start to enjoy the presence we bring for sharing spaces with others.

Marianne Williamson beautifully stated in her book *A Return to Love: Reflections on the Principles of A Course in Miracles,*

Our deepest fear is not that we are inadequate. Our deepest fear is that we are powerful beyond measure. It is our light, not our darkness that most frightens us. We ask ourselves, "Who am I to be brilliant, gorgeous, talented, fabulous?" Actually, who are you not to be? You are a child of God. Your playing small does not serve the world. There is nothing enlightened about shrinking so that other people won't feel insecure around you. We are all meant to shine, as children do. We were born to make manifest the glory of God that is within us. It's not just in some of us; it's in everyone. And as we let our own light shine, we unconsciously give other people permission to do the same. As we are liberated from our own fear, our presence automatically liberates others.

Somehow, we feel that if we hide our imperfections and only share our best selves, people will be much better off than when we are open about our inadequacies. However, in reality, the reverse seems to be the case. Living life to the fullest demands our vulnerability. Trying to live life in a shell does not benefit anybody except our selfish selves.

But once we live life through the lens of vulnerability, we benefit the world tremendously and liberate so many people by practicing openness with one another. I'm certain that we rob the world of our greatest potential when we fail to share our humanity with others.

I'm on a journey to share my story, hoping that by sharing my authentic self, I might enable people to gain insights that would help them commence their own vulnerability work. As

I stated at the beginning of this chapter, vulnerability work is a journey and not a destination. I'm still on it, and I have not yet arrived. I am not sure when I will. But I do know that my train has left the station. My vulnerability work will continue until I express all that is in me, when I will gladly say, "I have fought a good fight." Until then, the work continues.

Vulnerability work can scare some people away from us when they're not ready to learn about themselves. It can be an attractive feature in life that draws people to us in a quest to learn what makes us shine.

5

Being Myself

I was born and raised in Rensselaer, New York. At one time, Rensselaer was three villages—Greenbush, East Albany, and Bath—with a recent population of 9,471. Despite the small population in recent years, the town still has some of a big city's influence and culture. Over sixty years ago when I was growing up, my family lived modestly, as my father was a firm believer in hard work and modesty. When my dad passed away at age sixty-one, I was devastated because I'd been closely connected to him. He was my mentor, a role model, and so much more. In the silence of my heart, I see myself reading, *Be a Keeper* by an unknown author. A simple poem that I came across some years ago.

> One day a mother died. And on that clear, cold morning, In the warmth of her bedroom, The daughter was struck with The pain of learning that sometimes There isn't any more. No more hugs, No more lucky moments to celebrate together, No more phone calls just to chat, No more "just one minute." Sometimes, what we care about the most goes away. Never to return

before we can say good-bye, Say "I love you." So while we have it … it's best we love it … and care for it and fix it when it's broken and take good care of it when it's sick. This is true for marriage … And friendships … And children with bad report cards; And dogs with bad hips; And aging parents and grandparents; We keep them because they are worth it, Because we cherish them. Some things we keep—like a best friend that moves away or a classmate we grew up with. There are just some things that make us happy, no matter what. Life is important, and so are the people we know … And so, we keep them close. Be a Keeper!

While the pain of losing my father still remains, I am grateful to have shared those memorable years with him. I know some people whose fathers died much younger than mine did. I am gratified that I will live to see my sixty-sixth birthday, an age my father never had the opportunity to witness.

I used to wonder if I could ever live past sixty-one. That thought ran through my mind until I reached and passed that age. I will never get to measure whether that notion helped me to excel in life or hindered my growth. But I do know that the memory of the worry of never getting to see my sixty-first birthday was real to me. For that reason, I treasure every day I spend with my friends and family, along with the blessing of being able to give my time and resources to those I cherish and love.

As I've stated, I was raised in a lower-middle-class home where resources were limited but love for one another was apparent. My father, a hard worker, believed that hard work pays off and that a man ought to be the breadwinner and protector for the family. I learned firsthand what it means to be a working-class provider. Of course, such patriarchal settings bring their own challenges. It wasn't normal for a man to show emotions when I was growing up because it made him seem weak and vulnerable.

So I grew up with the same attitude. To make the situation worse, the guys in my neighborhood, my status as a New Yorker (which didn't make it any easier), the kids at school, and even colleagues in the workplace all validated that belief. But the longer I live and come closer to the realities of life, the clearer it is to me how important it is to be in touch with my emotions.

Expressing my emotions as a man was a learned behavior. I had to learn how to be me by allowing myself to be vulnerable without having the feeling of pride and social pressure to maintain a certain facade. As I have worked continuously to be more in touch with my emotions, I have read literature and other materials that educated me on the issues of vulnerability. The more I immersed myself in the process, the better I became.

Watching a YouTube video by social psychology professor Dr. Brené Brown titled "The Power of Vulnerability," which attracted about ten million viewers, validated my conviction about the reason why men should show more emotions and why showing vulnerability is healthy for humanity. There are so many advantages for men to be in touch with their feelings and still be men, so to speak. I have learned that the constructive expression of emotions is healthy for our well-being. So as not to overwhelm my readers, I will share a few advantages I have observed over the years that work for me in breaking down my internal walls.

I have learned that trying to maintain a certain facade of perfection toward the people around me can create a tremendous amount of pressure in my life. Our culture and society dictate these facades of perfection. If I don't take care, I find myself in that rabbit hole of phoniness that pushes me further away from being authentic and vulnerable. Conversely, being authentic can sometimes put me in a position of being vulnerable toward people around me.

Over time I have noticed that most people who have known me for some time have recognized a significant shift in my life. It feels good when I hear people telling me how a simple life experience, I shared with them has affected their lives. It further reveals to me how much impact a simple life experience shared with others can have to motivate them to pursue their own authentic selves. Being vulnerable around people who deserve my vulnerability builds courage and closeness to life. If we don't take care, the environment we find ourselves in can either restrict or liberate us from living an authentic life.

I realized the difference in cultures when I moved from the East Coast to the South and then the West Coast. People in the South and West were more accessible and friendlier compared to a certain New Yorkers, who have more aggressive personalities. I made a conscious decision to reevaluate myself. One of the adjustments I made was to be more open-minded with people and give them the benefit of the doubt. At first, it felt funny to me because I was leaving my comfort zone and trying something new. I began inviting my colleagues to Christmas parties at my house every year. My colleagues really bought the idea of spending time together outside of work. I used that opportunity to get to know my colleagues' families and what they enjoyed doing for fun, and they also enjoyed my family and openness to life.

On one particular occasion, my wife, Donna, organized a surprise birthday party for me. The invitees were both my friends and colleagues. I was surprised and humbled when people started pouring into our house. Donna, our children, and our guests were present as I opened each gift card and box and read them for everyone to hear.

At some point, I broke down out of joy and shed tears of appreciation for the overwhelming love that I had received. My experience beautifully expressed what Franklin P. Jones said about love. "Love doesn't make the world go around. Love is what makes the ride worthwhile."

Those little moments of vulnerability and authenticity make life more beautiful, and it felt good to sit with genuinely loving people and experience how everything unfolded organically, which truly shows how mutual energy attracts.

The popular saying "Like-minded people attract" is a true statement, especially when we use vulnerability as a virtue and a measuring stick. People attract others who feed and feel their presence. During my quest to discover myself, some persons I'd known for years couldn't fit in with the new me. It was disheartening to lose friends who weren't ready for the new adventure I had embarked on.

That doesn't necessarily mean they were bad people. It simply means that maybe they weren't ready for the journey or were a bit skeptical about it. I discovered that the journey of self-discovery can be unnerving to some people. That is, the destination isn't certain. The former is much safer than the latter because staying in the same space for so long makes us comfortable. But familiarity can result in mediocrity.

So this feeling of familiarity encourages us to connect with people who validate the very people that we have always been. Changing the narrative means shifting our perspective. The space between our old way of thinking and the new approach of reasoning is where vulnerability exists.

Vulnerability essentially has energy; energy does not discriminate. However, the way we channel our energy, whether negatively or positively, determines the result we'll get. That is, I can view vulnerability as a negative if I see it as a weakness, which literally translates the energy into defeat and pettiness. But if I view vulnerability as a positive force, that's how it will serve me.

The same principle applies when I start to make friends, moving from people who perceive vulnerability as a weakness to those who view vulnerability as a strength. Then the attraction becomes mutual. I must commit to listening to myself and believe in my decisions about this particular area of the project I'm working on in order to establish this new paradigm. Nothing can move me toward my desired direction like accepting myself as the agent of my own destiny. It's difficult to be vulnerable without the proper mental attitude when relating to one another and loving our partners. Love cannot flourish in an atmosphere of rigidity.

Loving someone requires being vulnerable, negotiating certain controls in our lives, and giving our partners access to a lot of things, such as admittance to our living spaces. Giving up control of our living spaces requires humility and vulnerability. Such a negotiation simply suggests to our partners that we trust them. That is, it would be difficult to tell people that we love them when we withhold both information and access, particularly qualities that should come naturally. Vulnerability lies in the midst of this decision.

The next clue that points to how much we love someone is giving that person access to our hearts. We must be honest and willing to share our inner truth and private information with our loved ones. It's a difficult feeling to open up to somebody who could crush or mock our intimate moments when we share these with them. Most relationships fail because of betrayal and lack of trust.

These two constructs—access to our living spaces and hearts—are only warranted when we are willing to give up control and become vulnerable in a situation. I believe that being vulnerable means having the courage to feel I am enough, no matter what happens in any situation. Knowing myself is a critical component of being vulnerable. It would be difficult for me to live an authentic life without knowing who I am and what makes me emotional.

Loving another person is first established by loving oneself. We measure how much we love ourselves by measuring how much we can love others. Do I love myself enough to be honest with myself, or do I love myself enough to sit in my pain, knowing that pain is part of a life experience and not a punishment? The list goes on.

If we can be vulnerable enough to admit these things, then it would be healthy to project the same thing to others. Love is fragile, not rigid. Love is open, not closed. Love is free, not reckless. Love is hard to find when we're rigid and closed up. These are the risks required to love and be vulnerable, but they are worth exploring.

I believe that some of the highlights discussed will help us to understand that our parentage usually determines how we see the world around us and that life's pain and suffering are in our DNA. We cannot escape them. The worst thing we can do to ourselves is to harbor our negative experiences in our minds, for such behavior can be toxic to our mental, emotional, and physical well-being and even determine the type of company we keep and how we express our love to our loved ones.

6

A Risky Enterprise

*B*eing alive is a risky enterprise. Staying alive is an even bigger challenge, and it is sometimes unpredictable, uncertain, dynamic, ongoing, stagnant, and fun. Life is largely unpredictable because we never know when an event might occur that will have a huge emotional impact on us, ranging from a child getting sick to witnessing a fatal accident on a freeway. Life is uncertain because it's risky to use the word *never* with absolute certainty. Life is dynamic because it can go from terrible to great unexpectedly. Imagine graduating from a college and hunting for a job for months, maybe even years, and you keep applying and eventually land in a position that could change your life. You may not consider it to be chance, but the dynamics make life interesting and ongoing.

The reverse might also be true. You have a great job. Then one day your services aren't needed anymore, or the company goes out of business or is bought out. At times, life feels stagnant, as though nothing exciting or new is happening. At other moments, it's fun and energizing.

In all these instances, life seems risky because it's constantly changing, which is the very definition of life. This ongoing change can make one feel vulnerable. I am certain that life persists despite these unexpected twists and turns.

So life is a risky enterprise. A risk-free life is no life at all. Only the dead are risk-free. Even though the world is a risky space, this doesn't mean that I should stop living. I should live in spite of the warning signs. I should be vulnerable enough to experience and enjoy myself. It all starts the moment that I wake up and get out of bed.

I learn every day that I must show up on a daily basis, ready to take a shot at life. While I am aware of the twists and turns every day can bring, I still choose to take the risk of living life to the fullest, and I inspire others to do the same because we only have one shot at life every day.

When I travel around the country speaking to my associates, I make myself vulnerable onstage by telling personal stories with the hope of connecting with my audience and helping them open up to life's possibilities. Life is a risky enterprise because it requires a lot of unconscious and conscious decisions—negotiations of a sort—and the act of being vulnerable at least once per day. When I acknowledged that life is a risky enterprise, it made a world of difference to me, especially concerning relationships, whether professional or personal.

When my associates approach me for advice or an executive decision in a professional setting, giving them my time and undivided attention is the least I can do. It's about taking a chance to listen to another person who needs our attention; being present and making another person feel heard; giving someone an opportunity to be able to express the urgency in the present discussion; encouraging a person to know he or she matters; and honoring humanity by taking a chance to listen to a person who reached out for an audience.

In my personal relationships, I am aware that what I do on

a daily basis can affect my loved ones and me. The knowledge and admission of that alone is a risky enterprise because I never know wholly how things may turn out, but taking the risk every day makes it more meaningful.

Some years back, I communicated with a young Midwestern author via email. I had read her book and loved her narrative about her experience in Kenya as a program director of an orphanage. She went to Kenya for charity work and fell in love with the whole experience. I was particularly touched when she mentioned how her parents traveled with her to share her experience. While her parents weren't particularly intrigued with the idea of traveling to a foreign land, they understood what that meant to their daughter and decided to take the risk to support her. In the author's email correspondence, she noted,

> The experience of having my Mom and Dad come to Kenya is one of the biggest gifts they could EVER have given to me. I don't think they will ever be able to give me a bigger, more meaningful, more precious gift than sharing in the excitement of my life here in Kenya.

As a parent, the author's remarks resonated with me. I took a similar trip with my daughter to Africa. It was a special day in her life, and the family wanted to celebrate with her.

We asked her, "What do you want for your special day?"

She replied, "I want a trip to Morocco with just you, dad."

Initially, I wasn't sure what to make of her request for several reasons. Although she had been to Africa many times, we hadn't, so I wasn't sure what to expect. But for the love of my children and my desire for them to travel the world and experience life, I agreed that she and I would go to Morocco together.

We thoroughly enjoyed the experience. We must have taken over a thousand photos, including images of when we went to the market and the locals invited us to carry a live snake. It was terrifying and nerve-racking, but we did it and had fun with the experience. The overwhelming hospitality we received from the locals was heartwarming.

I am convinced that living a full and meaningful existence requires taking calculated risks. Venturing into a new situation can be frightening, but once we expose ourselves to a new way of learning and experiencing life, whether it's traveling, relating to completely different cultures, or remaining open to life's possibilities, we'll never be the same again. So life is a risk worth taking. The great jurist, Oliver Wendell Holmes Jr., eloquently said, "A mind that is stretched by a new experience can never go back to its old dimensions."

Our daughter literally stretched my mind by exposing my thinking to a new way of seeing the world through the lenses of the Moroccans. I must add that our Moroccan experience was made possible because, as a father, I chose to take the chance of traveling to a foreign land in Africa, even though that might not have been my first choice. That simple decision to take the chance opened my eyes and mind to other possibilities life could offer—an opportunity to see the world differently and a different way of being.

The Moroccan experience has made me a better human being. Experiencing how people in Morocco live and relate to one another, taking life at face value, and living in the now were some of the things I learned from that trip. I have occasionally wondered if there was any way I could have measured the encounter I would have missed had I denied myself the opportunity to experience Morocco with my daughter.

It's clear to me that it's easier to measure our Moroccan

visit because we went, but it's difficult to measure what we have never become or experienced. The same principle applies to how we measure life. I can only measure my life by what I do and how I do things, because life is movement.

In this context, I include the steps I took to resign from my comfortable job and move to join a cell tower company and the steps I took to stand in front of hundreds of people to talk about leadership, compassion, empathy, acceptance, diversity, and a host of other transformational subjects that motivate and improve businesses one mind at a time. These are some of the ways that I measure my life.

I am certain that subtle gestures along the way, such as conversing with people on subways, helping people find their way, and simply smiling at a stranger on the streets, also measure my life. Each gesture is risky by itself and requires some level of vulnerability in order to take a chance.

I have no regrets for how I have lived my life. Regrets are simply manifestations of an unfulfilled life. Always looking back on my life and recalling my failures from a place of self-pity perpetuates the "not enough" feeling. But reviewing my past and using my struggles and mistakes as catalysts for becoming who I am today benefits me and the world more because regrets don't fix anything at all; rather, they push me into an emotional paralysis.

Entertaining mistakes and challenges of any sort are the true definitions of life, which is why it is a risky enterprise. Admitting that life is a risky enterprise shows vulnerability in itself, and it takes courage to be vulnerable. It has been a liberating exercise for me since I began this work in vulnerability and authenticity.

Being alive is a risky enterprise; staying alive is an even bigger risk. Also, a risk-free life is no life at all because only the dead are risk-free. But as long as we venture into a new way of living, though it could be frightening, it is rewarding as well. It's difficult to measure a life by what we have never become or experience; therefore, we should face our challenges. We should not live a life of regrets, because remorse is simply a manifestation of an unfulfilled life.

7

A Liberating Exercise

*W*hat is the work to be done? I have always asked myself this question when people with life-challenging situations confront me. Starting an event with a question allows me to find the work that needs to be done. I also use the same approach to solve my own life's challenges. A work that needs to be done could be as basic as listening. In other words, don't say a word; instead, actively listen to what a person, a group, or your heart is saying. Or it can be as fundamental as asking an individual, "How do you need me to assist you?"

Offering our time, energy, and presence and being true to ourselves or others makes a world of a difference to whatever situation is at hand. Such an exercise simply suggests to me that I do matter to myself. It also suggests to others who want to engage me in their issues that they matter too. On the flip side, it's just as important to be vulnerable enough to disclose my own issues to my close friends and family members. But it's most rewarding when I am a mirror to others' issues and challenges, when I can see myself in other people's struggles and can connect with others on human levels, no matter one's age, spiritual beliefs, social status, and so on.

Let me use this relatively generic example to illustrate my

point. As a father of five wonderful children, I learned this firsthand while raising them. Sometimes my children would burst into the living room with concern and frustration written all over their faces. Filtering through what they were saying and identifying the real problems required some level of active listening by asking myself, *What is the work to be done in this situation?*

It's very difficult to truly understand my children's concerns when I am distracted and inattentive. Asking "What is the work to be done?" with a distracted mind probably worsens the situation. So learning how to identify when my mind is distracted was important. One of the ways to quickly check whether I was focused and listening was to mindfully observe what I was doing as the children were talking to me.

Watching a car show on the television and never blinking while the children were sharing their concerns meant I was distracted. But if I turned off or muted the TV to give them attention, that meant I was focused on them. At that moment, this action demonstrated two things to the children: they mattered, and I cared enough to listen to them.

I must admit that I had to learn how to listen to people because I suspect that I could have attention-deficit disorder (ADD). Paying attention doesn't come naturally for me. I need to checking my emotions and be vulnerable at that moment.

Being vulnerable around my loved ones is critical for me. It's important to me because it allows them to feel and witness humanity in action. It simply means being aware of my feelings, feeling free to express them without the fear of being judged, and giving others permission to be vulnerable too, if they wish.

I view vulnerability work as an ongoing exercise. There's no graduation date; instead it's a continuous effort to be the best me that I can become. I view being vulnerable as a liberating exercise to give myself permission to be me, especially knowing that holding back negative emotions about how people will perceive me if they know where I have been and what I have done can cause unhealthy stresses in my life. It's a personal quest and a decision to commit to a vulnerability journey.

While being vulnerable may sound liberating, it requires courage in order to express itself. I told a story previously about how walking away from my comfortable job in New York to move to another new job was initially a stretch for my family and me. It took courage and deliberate action to take the risk to make it happen. In this liberating exercise, I am convinced that courage leads to vulnerability and vulnerability leads to action or inaction. Action or inaction is the final stage of the three:

Courage + Vulnerability = Action or Inaction

It's difficult to measure courage or vulnerability without the action or inaction component. How a person is feeling translates either into action or into inaction. Action, for example, was my ability to resign from my comfortable job to relocate and pursue my passion, which at that time meant a pay cut. However, inaction would have been not to resign and thus mute my passion. Fortunately, I took the option of picking up courage, venturing into the unknown, and moving on. This simple but uncertain shift gave me so much confidence to embrace the idea that courage plus vulnerability equals action.

Looking back, I realized that without even knowing it, I had thought through my decision of resigning and relocating to Arizona through the lens the question, "What is the work to be done?" It's a loaded inquiry because it would have been difficult to take a chance or make a calculated move without identifying the work to be done. I knew I needed to do more and be more in life, but most importantly, I needed to be in a place where I could be more independent and influential. Unfortunately, my position at my former company in New York did not allow me to live my passion, so with courage, I took a chance and acted.

Since we've relocated, I am now living my passion. As part of my dream to help others achieve their dreams, I incorporated motivational, transformative, and self-help components into my training speeches, encouraging people to live life and not just exist. I find the exercise of identifying those hidden treasures in my life very liberating and exciting.

To make a conscious decision to be true to self takes courage and intentionality of purpose. Being self-aware means understanding why we do what we do and the way we do it. Self-awareness is a lifelong journey that has no ending. The quest to discover ourselves and our purpose can lead us to explore our options, such as who to establish relationships with, where to live, how to dress, which school to go to, and so on.

If we really look at our choices, they directly reflect everything about us. I deepened my sense of self when I embarked on facing my realities. Growing up as a teenager, I lacked self-confidence, which really affected my self-image. I couldn't pinpoint the exact reason why, but along the way, a friend kept reminding me of the potential I possessed. It was difficult for me to accept because I was not seeing myself the way my friend saw me.

Because of this distorted self-view, it took me a long time to accept myself for who I was and what I could become. Once I realized that people saw me the way I perceived myself, I started to treat myself better, dress confidently, and think differently. I realized that I am enough. All that I want and will ever be is within me. I need no validation from anyone to make me feel whole. I am enough.

I want to emphasize that asking a simple question—What's

the work to be done?—allows us to focus on the issue at hand without wandering off into other issues. Finding that answer will help answer the other questions we have. And the only way to identify the issue is to pay attention, which requires intense listening and focus. When we courageously ask questions, pay attention, and remain vulnerable enough to admit our shortcomings, then we can take the bold action needed.

Part III

Forgiveness

8

It Won't Happen to Me

A video on YouTube, "No Handshake for You" (Kevin 2009), depicted an incident that occurred when the US president at the time visited Great Britain. As the president and British prime minister (PM) walked into 10 Downing Street, the president shook hands with the police officer on duty, but when the officer stretched out his hand to the PM, the leader ignored him and walked on. It was an awkward and embarrassing moment that was broadcast on national and global platforms.

Although we could minimize the negative effect it might have had on the police officer, what do you think the officer was thinking or feeling? On an intellectual level, the officer could rationalize why the PM refused to shake his hand; it might not have been common practice for the PM to shake hands with the officer. However, on an emotional level, the officer might have felt crushed and humiliated. Thus, forgiving the PM in this context could happen in two ways, on both intellectual and emotional levels.

Forgiveness as a construct has presence, whether we are receiving it from someone we have offended or giving it to someone who has offended us. Our nonverbal actions govern how other people think and feel about us, but do our nonverbal actions govern how we think and feel about ourselves? Evidence shows that they do (Cuddy 2012).

This claim resonates with me because forgiveness does not come easily for me, and it is usually obvious when I encounter someone I have not forgiven. My body language gives me away, especially when I get emotional. Sometimes I like to believe that because I'm very mindful of my environment and treat people fairly, individuals will not purposefully hurt my feelings. However, I have quickly realized over the years that this is simply not the case.

Though I have tried hard to forgive easily when I'm offended (and expect people to forgive me when I offend them), the truth is that it can be very challenging to forgive someone who offends us. Even years later, we may still carry hurt feelings from how our first partners made us feel. Our memories and emotional triggers are part of our human makeup. I now recognize that as long as I live, people will always offend me directly or indirectly, and I will do the same to others. Realizing this equips me with the ability to entertain forgiveness at both the intellectual and emotional levels.

On the intellectual level, I find it easier to forgive. Obviously, from a logical perspective, we practice how to show up and deliver effectively because our bodies shape our minds and our minds shape our bodies (Cuddy 2012). We know that if we condition our bodies to show certain positive gestures in public, then we can act as if we have forgiven our offenders. In other words, we can memorize how we want to behave in public, and over time, we can master that behavior.

So on an intellectual level, we do very well in public because we rehearse our lines effectively and mindfully. We learn how to master our craft by practicing over and over again, reading materials that relate to the topic, or watching videos that educate us with visuals. So it is evident how to forgive on an intellectual level. But what do we do when we want to forgive someone on an emotional level?

On an emotional level, I feel jaded when I get to know people's shortcomings. If someone lies to me in order to take something from me, it is difficult for me to forgive such a person because I feel manipulated. On an intellectual level, I know forgiveness sets me free. But on an emotional level, I find it difficult to let go. Because our feelings are connected to our beliefs, I can connect this chapter back to the acceptance chapter: "acceptance means so much to me that I do whatever it takes to waste time to get what I want." But in forgiveness work, I cannot make someone forgive me unless that person wants to. It is out of my control to make someone forgive me. Sharing my perspective is one of the reasons why I'm writing this book.

There are two ways to handle forgiveness work: choose to forgive or not. Both choices have consequences, either positive or negative. Self-forgiveness is the most important part of forgiveness because unresolved intrapersonal anger and toxic bitterness adversely affect health. For forgiveness to be whole and operative, it has to be emotion-focused, with the intention to overcome negative mood states such as anger, anxiety, depression, and guilt (Wilson et al. 2008).

While reading scientific journal articles on forgiveness, I have found that the concept of the toxicity related to unforgiveness seems believable. Health-related issues are among the consequences of not forgiving. To a certain degree, I have experienced the potential consequences of unforgiveness, and it becomes necessary to do forgiveness work to ensure that cognitive and moral work are in sync. In other words, our thought process has to involve reflecting on positive experiences in order to produce healthy results, and our mood has to reflect stability so we can reap emotional and medical health benefits (Wilson et al. 2008).

I have realized that if I fail to forgive myself or anyone who offends me, I am positioning myself for a toxic, health-related catastrophe. Failing to forgive is unhealthy and can be deadly if not resolved. Unforgiveness can lead to depression, anger, anxiety, and guilt (Wilson et al. 2008). I find myself making a conscious effort to forgive myself for not letting go on an emotional level and forgiving others who have offended me. The idea that "it can never happen to me" is a false affirmation, for at some point in our lives, we will offend others, and others will offend us. So let us accept this reality and seek ways to make things right with ourselves so we might make things right with others. Life is an echo, for what we release into the universe is what comes back to us. The belief that we reap what we sow is universal. So the choice is mine, whether to forgive for my health's sake or not.

I welcome you to reason with me that forgiveness occurs on both mental and emotional levels and that it has to be emotion-focused, with the intention to overcome negative mood states such as anger, anxiety, depression, and guilt. The best place to start forgiveness work is with ourselves, for it's a personal quest. It is never easy, but it is necessary.

9

I Do Have a Choice

*F*orgiveness is a choice. It is the choice to forgive or not. Nobody can make us forgive ourselves or others. The power to do so is exclusively ours. It is very tempting to seek revenge rather than walk away from a person or society that offends us, especially knowing the temptations associated with revenge. To an extent, revenge can make us feel justified. In other words, we may feel entitled to seek revenge. For example, when people offend us and others hear about it and sympathize with us, it would be reasonable to think that people would support us if we decided to seek revenge. This entitlement mentality makes us feel empowered to hold grudges against those who offend us. Unfortunately, if we're not strong-willed, we can easily fall into pleasing others by responding the exact way they expect us to respond (not forgiving). It takes guts and vulnerability to forgive others.

Forgiveness is not a checklist. In fact, forgiveness will never happen without our permission. Nobody can do forgiveness work on our behalf; it's exclusively our right to decide whether to forgive or not. This chapter is about self-reflection as it relates to forgiveness, both internally as an observer and externally as the observed. Introspectively, we ask the question, how forgiving are we, either as a group or as a person? It can be an uncomfortable question because asking about how forgiving we are challenges our consciousness. It takes a person of character to dig for the real answer. Externally (viewing ourselves from the outside), how do we see ourselves? Do we view ourselves as people who are capable of forgiving or not? The choice is ours to make.

Once we realize that forgiveness is a choice and not a checklist, we have furthered our work on forgiveness. True forgiveness comes when we view forgiving others as a choice. How we decide to show up on a daily basis determines how that day will turn out. We can apply the same principle on how or who to forgive today. Forgiveness is personal and revealing. It's personal because we get to choose how to go about forgiving or even whether to forgive at all. It's revealing because it speaks about our spiritual character. The way we forgive or fail to forgive others determines the type of people we are and the choices we make.

I'm certain that the way we forgive ourselves reflects the way we forgive others. For example, one major dramatic event in our lives that led us to unforgiveness or forgiveness could cause us to relocate to a different state or country, and by relocating we open a new door in our lives that couldn't have been had the event not occured. In our new place of residence, we might go to a new school, make new friends, and possibly find a soul mate, all as a result of one single decision to relocate because of a particular event.

The result of one single act of forgiveness or unforgiveness could be a major shift in our lives. Interestingly, we will never know whom we could have become if we had made a different choice, but it is very important to know whom we have chosen to become because of it. Whatever happens in the course of life, knowing we do have a choice when it comes to forgiveness is critical.

I'm certainly sure that we should not go through life with regrets. A life of "could have, should have, would have" is one of wasted energy and time. Regret can be an indication that we are not content, whole, or satisfied about our past, present, or future. But if we live our lives knowing that we are where we are today is a result of our choices, then there is no need to live in regret; instead, we can make changes and move on with our lives. The same thing is applicable with choosing to whether to forgive. If we choose not to forgive, let's also be willing to accept whatever consequences that are associated with that choice.

On the contrary, choosing to forgive has its rewards and consequences as well, but let us not go through life wishing it away without making a choice or a decision. Sitting on the fence leaves us uncertain in some other areas of our lives. But if we recognize the experience and make a clear choice to forgive or not forgive, then we can better face the consequences of our choices, both physically and emotionally.

Emotional toxicity could be an indication of unforgiveness, especially in a group setting. One researcher called it emotional terrorism when 22 percent of employees in a particular organization applied for transfers due to intolerable conflict, backbiting behavior, and a culture of intolerance (Goleman 2008). If we internalize such symptoms without taking any action, then they can become toxic to our health and systems. In this instance, working in a toxic environment is unhealthy for the individual or organization. So for an employee to move on, they have to exercise self-forgiveness for allowing themselves to be abused by management and then take necessary action to stop the toxicity, whether this means transferring to a different department or site or reporting to a higher authority in the organization. It's never a good idea to work in a toxic environment. Choices are always available. We just have to look closer and intentionally.

Looking closely might entail asking some questions, such as:

- Why am I feeling this way about this particular situation?
- What's the root cause of this situation?
- Why am I allowing myself to feel this way?

Choosing to start the work with personal questions could lead to closer and more accurate answers. Intentionality of purpose is also critical in decision-making. For example, what am I trying to accomplish in this particular situation? How do I approach the circumstance? Am I willing to face the truth about it even if it is not in my favor?

Walking into a situation prepared deflates so many tensions and uncertainties. If we make a choice to forgive someone (or not) with a clear objective, the result usually makes sense in the end. On the other hand, a distorted thought process generally produces a distracted result. So when it comes to whether to forgive or not, we always have choices. Let's decide wisely.

Forgiving someone wholeheartedly has always been a challenge for me. But I'm a work in progress. To forgive or not is a phenomenon that plagues everyone. It is good to know that forgiveness is a choice. Only the person who wants to forgive has the exclusive right to do so, even in the case of forgiving ourselves. The way we forgive ourselves and others reflects who we are as a whole. If we want to measure how someone lives his or her life, we should observe how that person forgive him- or herself and others, for forgiveness is a choice. Also, learning that emotional toxicity could be a sign of unforgiveness is refreshing. We need an emotional cleansing every now and then.

10

Never Forgive Enough

*F*orgiveness is defined as a conscious, deliberate decision to release feelings of resentment or vengeance toward a person or group who has harmed you, regardless of whether they actually deserve your forgiveness (Hicks 2018). This definition sums up the very essence of practicing forgiveness. We don't forgive because the person who offends us deserves it; rather, it's for the sake of letting go of the thoughts that sap our energy.

One event that depicts the practice of forgiveness is Reginald Denny's story. During the 1992 Los Angeles riots, four rioters pulled Reginald, an innocent passerby, from his truck and nearly beat him to death. Reginald ended up suffering from permanent nerve damage, impaired vision, and a constant ringing in his ears. What made Reginald's story so compelling was that he totally forgave, without any expectations, the rioters who almost beat him to death. If Reginald could forgive those who attempted to kill him, I'm morally obligated to forgive those who offend me.

To look deeper into Reginald's story, I realized that sometimes we fail to forgive others because of public or friends' opinions about what happened to us, not because of what they did to us. In Reginald's case, it would have been justifiable for him to seek revenge or retaliation, but he chose to forgive instead.

It was a big lesson for me to learn that forgiving those who offend us is possible with no strings attached. I believe that conscious or intentional forgiveness is more powerful than withholding forgiveness because of public opinion. Reginald decided to forgive his attackers for the sake of his peace of mind. He made a conscious decision to let go of all the other reasons why he shouldn't forgive.

Another act of forgiveness that I found incredibly inspiring involved the parents of two-year-old Lane Graves, who forgave Disney after an alligator killed their toddler son at a Disney property. Lane's parents believed that suing Disney would not bring their child back; instead, they channeled their energy into opening a charity foundation for their child and the future health of the family. Lane's parents evidently channeled their frustration and energy into something positive as opposed to seeking a lawsuit. My heart goes out to the parents who lost their child and Reginald Denny. Both suffered tragedy yet were able to rise above their misfortunes.

Reginald Denny and the Graves had one thing in common. Reginald Denny shifted his thought process from the violence committed against him to the root cause of the incident. In his interview, he shared more about what led to the violence as opposed to how he was brutally beaten. Invariably, once he shifted his mind-set to the root cause, he started to see the whole picture instead of fractions of the story. It dawned on me that sometimes we tend to focus on a fraction of an event rather than the whole tale. And once we act based on the fraction, we end up not totally forgiving our transgressors. But when we act out of compassion and empathy, we allow ourselves to see the big picture. Reginald saw beyond his pain and shed light on others' pain.

Lane's parents rose above their pain when they decided not to sue Disney. They said, "Disney has already gone to great lengths to make sure something like this won't happen again—removing hundreds of alligators from its lakes and putting up a lot of warning signs. So, what is money going to bring?" (Riley 2016). They showed total forgiveness without expectations and exercised compassion and empathy without minimizing the loss of their child.

Though years have passed since these events, we're still discussing their pain and responses to their suffering, which suggests to me that forgiveness takes time. "Automatic forgiveness can hide great resentment and even hatred for the enemy; it is a slow process; it takes a lifetime" (University Wire 2016).

Forgiving someone is not an overnight practice. It takes time, and during that period of forgiveness, it is possible some person might offend us in more ways. If we're busy keeping records of how many times the same person has offended us, we'll probably never forgive that individual. So it is important to recognize that forgiveness takes time and, in the process, we may be offended again. Thus, patience is critical when we want to forgive others.

Forgiving others is easier to do if we can remember when we need to be pardoned (Amsden 1997). We're as guilty as the next person who offends us. To be able to forgive others who offend us, we should learn how to be empathetic (put ourselves in someone's shoes). Think about it this way: How many times have we offended our parents, siblings, spouses, friends, and so on?

The same principle applies to all of us who have a holier-than-thou mentality and can't forgive others. Think again.

None of us deserve to be forgiven if we're busy holding grudges and keeping a record of those who have offended us. What goes through our minds when we offend someone and they stubbornly refuse to forgive us? Do we understand why they feel the way they do, or do we demand forgiveness? I think the latter is more realistic, but above all else, forgiving those who offend us is always a better choice.

It is healthier to forgive our transgressors within six weeks than to hold grudges for a lifetime. Holding grudges for a long period of time increases our heart rate and raises our blood pleasure, boosting the likelihood of heart disease (Amsden 1997). So for the sake of our health, forgiveness is a necessity.

Additionally, when we learn how to forgive, we get to keep our smiles and happiness. I'm certain that forgiving our transgressors also helps to improve our focus. I have noticed that the more I practice forgiving others, the more time I have to concentrate on things that matter to me.

My children are my world, and I'll do anything to stay focused on what matters to them and their future. For me to continue having a positive outlook on life, I must do whatever it takes to get rid of any negative energy within me, including unforgiveness, so I may stay happy and smiling for my lovely family members and myself. I've realized that, with this mindset, forgiveness shouldn't be biased. In other words, if I have the capacity to forgive my loved ones multiple times, I can do the same with all human beings.

I realize how difficult and unrealistic forgiving everyone may sound, but it's necessary for wholeness and authenticity. The six-week rule is a tough one for me to live by because it's unrealistic for me to think that I have ever forgiven anybody within six weeks of being offended. But I'm a work in progress.

Doing forgiveness work has taught me that "forgiveness

should not just be perceived as a spiritual cleansing but also as a physical and emotional well-being" (Agbanyim 2013). There are physical indicators of a person who practices forgiveness. The person is more at peace as well as relaxed, calm, and confident. When we know that everything under the sun passes away, it should be a source of hope that forgiving one more person is a total forgiveness without any expectations. Forgiveness promotes psychological healing through positive changes. We should be able to concentrate on what matters in life as opposed to carrying the baggage of unforgiveness.

Forgiveness is more beneficial when it's intrapersonal rather than interpersonal. When we forgive someone from the bottom of our hearts—not because of pressure from family, friends, or the community—it has a more lasting effect. It is a coping strategy that victims use to overcome the negative emotional state that comes with unforgiveness (Raj and Wiltermuth 2016). Practicing forgiveness is a healthy way of living. By not practicing forgiveness, we are not practicing love toward one another.

I purposefully kept this chapter short to invite my readers to ponder over what has been discussed, especially having given two real-life stories of individuals who experienced injustice but still forgave their transgressors. Forgiveness has a long-lasting impact on our lives.

I also discussed the benefits of forgiveness to both the victim and the transgressor. The victim forgives to gain spiritual, physical, psychological, and emotional benefits while the transgressor should learn how to be human even in the face of injustice.

Part IV

Compassion

11

It Can Happen to Me

*C*ompassion from friends and family have filled my life. The more I think about compassion, the more I remember how people have contributed to my life, those whose help I least expected to receive and others who rightly fit the role. I wouldn't be where I am today if not for people who instilled hope into my life. I'm a living testament to the power of compassion at work. I must also mention that the challenges I have experienced have helped make me who I am today. So my life has been a reflection of human experience.

Compassion has always been viewed as a sympathetic consciousness of others' distress, together with a desire to alleviate it (Merriam-Webster 2018). I have had my fair share of people reaching out to assist me through words of encouragement, financial assistance, or offers of presence. There have been too many times to count. I'll attempt to highlight some instances that I can recall, with the hope that sharing these stories will help you remember and appreciate yours as well.

I always love interacting with people because it energizes me to have human connections and experiences. I enjoy sharing my stories with people, and I am delighted to hear others' stories too. I wasn't always a social person, but I eventually noticed the enormous benefits of storytelling, both in the workplace and in social gatherings, particularly while visiting our different corporate offices to see how each office is handling our corporate business plans.

Over the last fifteen months, I have visited our different corporate locations nearly fifty-two times across the United States. This means I'm constantly in the air at least three times a month with little rest. During these travels, I have made it a point to interact with all my associates to ensure I make contact with them and listen to their concerns and triumphant stories. The rewards for connecting with my team members are immeasurable. One of the benefits is that I, as well as my associates, are inspired and engaged at work, and they hold each other accountable in good spirits.

On one occasion, I received an email from an associate expressing how grateful she was for my contributions to our company and humanity. She mentioned that she understood why people always wanted to be around me. She highlighted her concern about how I had mentioned in one of my speeches how sometimes, I get a little tired. Her candid expression caught my attention. "I hope you give yourself permission to rest, dear one, because everyone will ultimately benefit from it enormously."

Her remark and honest concern humbled me because she didn't have to share her observations about me, but she did it out of shared concern. It reminded me that showing compassion in the workplace can transform and humanize the work environment. It also creates a healthy communication link between authority figures and associates in the workplace. Showing compassion in the workplace promotes job performance and helps individuals to recognize the truth that people often carry pain from their personal lives into work (Aboul-Ela 2017). By recognizing this truth, we realize that our roles in organizations, social settings, or relationships do not shield us from experiencing human suffering. Our titles don't exempt us from facing the work that is right in front of us. We are human in spite of our titles.

Our roles in board meetings, our families, or our friendships are separate from who we are as individuals. Those roles are merely a manifestation of what drives us, not who we are. Sometimes we become disoriented when we think we're the roles that we play on a daily basis. Our roles are just that: roles. They don't showcase the core existence of our humanity; rather, they're a performance that measures our levels of responsibilities. Our core humanity is to show love, happiness, joy, forgiveness, acceptance, vulnerability, and compassion to one another. If we can understand that we're not the roles we perform on a daily basis, then we can live as individuals and not the roles we play. I know this firsthand because I experience it on a daily basis.

As a father and husband, my role is to love, provide for, and protect my family. To play these roles effectively, I have to be human about it and understand that patience is required in all relationships. Having children is one thing; being present for them is another. And that's where compassion comes in.

As a brother, I have to regularly check on my siblings and maintain healthy relationships with them. To be able to do so, I have to be human about it, knowing we will argue sometimes but always love one another no matter what. Maintaining such relationships requires showing compassion. A biological link inextricably binds us together, and my job as a brother is to do whatever it takes to love my siblings.

As a son, my responsibility was to care for my parents. Now that they're not physically with me, I carry them with me in my mind wherever I go, for they are my rock, and I miss them every day of my life. I see myself every now and then talking about my parents to people around me, which shows the strong bond and connection that existed between us.

As a corporate authority figure, I'm responsible for thousands of associates, many of whom indirectly report to me, but I'm also committed to their welfare as part of my corporate obligations. This includes making sure they're treated fairly in the workplace and are provided for with the necessary training, tools and encouragement. A healthy workforce is a healthy society.

As a friend, I have to look out for my friends and support them as needed. I remember my decades-old friends who gave me valuable lessons that I will never forget. One of my friends (now deceased) told me that I would become somebody very important in the society, and he encouraged me to be confident in myself and pursue my dreams. Those words stay with me through tough times and help me overcome life's difficulties. I will recall his advice as long as I live. He was a great friend, and I miss his friendship.

This is not an exhaustive list of the roles many of us occupy on a daily basis; others include, for example, uncle, aunt, teacher, mentor, and so many others. In truth, we are not the roles we play; rather, we're human beings who happen to assume these roles by virtue of so many variables, some of which were chosen for us by our parents, ancestors, and birthplaces.

The only thing that remains constant in all these roles is that we're all human beings having human experiences. I believe, if we can view our existence through the lens of our humanity, we can then start to realize that what happens to us directly can affect others indirectly. And by virtue of recognizing our shared humanity, we can start to develop compassion for one another. We must practice showing compassion on a daily basis. Compassion work is never a one-time practice.

My views about my life have been shaped by so many people who showed me compassion through their deeds, including my associate who reminded me to get some rest from work, and by life experiences that have humbled me to show compassion to others. It's important to know that our work titles and roles don't define our humanity; rather, the core of who we are does, such as having compassion, forgiving others, showing vulnerability, being brave in the face of challenges, and accepting those who might not fit our pedigree. Our humanity is conflicted once we start to view ourselves as our roles.

Finally, once we understand that human struggles are universal, then we can start showing genuine compassion to one another, whether in the boardroom, at home, in social settings, or among strangers, because just as we give compassion, we also need it.

12

How Do I Want to Be Treated?

I watched a *Britain's Got Talent* show this year, and it compelled me to think more deeply about how compassion begets a radical candor. A contestant, Gruffydd Wyn Roberts, was visibly nervous when he was called on stage to sing. He was so nervous that he performed poorly, even though he had it in him to sing wonderfully.

As he started to sing, his flat, uncoordinated voice prompted Simon, one of the judges, to interrupt him. Simon was brutally honest when he expressed to the contestant that his performance was "cold," without any energy to the song. Simon then asked the contestant to let go of his nervousness and sing with warmth.

At this point, Simon asked the contestant if he had another song to present. The contestant stated that he could sing a different song of his choice. Before he started to sing his new song, Simon encouraged him to drink a glass of water.

To the audience's amazement, the contestant picked up courage and momentum and sang the song exceptionally well. This performance led to a golden buzzer, meaning that the contestant's performance exceeded the judges' and audience's expectations, prompting the judges to select him among other contestants to skip the process and be placed at the top of the list for the next round of the contest.

The video was exceptional because it demonstrated to me how we can uplift others who are having challenges in one area or another. Using the contest illustration as a case in point, Simon expressed radical candor to the contestant out of compassion because he had confidence in him. To everyone's amazement, and with their encouragement and support, the contestant excelled.

I have been using this approach for years without knowing a term for it, but this video put it in perspective for me. I find myself self-reflecting on a question, such as, "If I'm in the contestant's shoes, how do I want to be treated?" As cold as the judge was initially to the contestant, I would rather have someone tell me the truth than deceptively sugarcoat it. It's my observation that the majority of the conflicts in the workplace, at home, or in social settings are rooted in a lack of radical candor. When we fail to be honest with one another, we perpetuate the very things (disingenuousness, deception, etc.) that we're trying to avoid. In particular, we miss an opportunity to make an observation on the spot.

Being radically candid means, one is becoming an agent of change in real time. For example, Simon made the observation in real time by providing constructive criticism to the contestant.

It does not matter what performance someone is trying to give. Once we observe it and feel like giving feedback, it's important to make the observations positively and from a place of compassion rather than with a negative attitude. In the workplace, I make sure I engage my team members or associates in candid conversations, allowing us to be open-minded and present without any fear of repercussions.

On a few occasions, new associates who had never met me

before were amazed when they felt no hierarchical pressures or differences upon meeting me for the first time. It's a deliberate effort on my part to ensure that everybody is treated equally, irrespective of rank or expertise, because in the final analysis, we are all individuals having shared human experiences.

I have passed down this idea to my immediate colleagues in an effort to make our work environment accommodating, satisfying, engaging, friendlier, and productive. I believe in the golden rule, or treating others the way we want to be treated. Because of this mind-set, I'm constantly looking for ways to promote healthy human relationships. Author Kim Scott's book gave me a new approach to developing healthy human relationships in the workplace. She believes "to be a good boss you have to Care Personally at the same time you Challenge Directly" (Scott 2017).

Caring doesn't mean losing our humanity. We train those we care about, so to practice leadership, we should inspire by caring for those we're leading. Experts in the fields of neuroscience, pediatrics, education, psychology, and psychiatry have proven that empathy and caring are essential parts of human health (Szalavitz and Perry 2011).

Caring for one another is a critical component in human relationships, and people can sense when we don't care about them, whether in the workplace, at home, or in social settings. To practice caring is to promote healthy human relationships; caring is the core of every relationship. If we use the analogy of caring for a child, we realize that it takes compassion or empathy to raise a child because we were once children ourselves. Therefore, we can relate to the experience.

Caring for an elderly or ill family member also requires compassion. The outlook needed for such care is learned and rehearsed repeatedly. The same sequence applies in the workplace in order to extend compassion to our team members. For a company to function optimally, it must have managers who are measured by how they treat their team members and how committed they are to staying in their truth as a powerful weapon (White 1998). An uncommitted manager is likely to have unstable team members. I'm persuaded that it takes compassion to become an exceptional leader. Without it, practicing humanity is challenging.

It is difficult to practice compassion and disengagement at the same time, for either we care or we don't. Both constructs can't be practiced simultaneously. I made a conscious decision to show compassion to humanity, for I desire for others to treat me with compassion. Showing compassion to one another is a choice and a practice. To practice compassion means being considerate of the sufferings and feelings of those we encounter, either in person or virtually, for the practice of compassion knows no boundaries. A compassionate leader is someone who hears or reads about a team member who's undergoing serious challenges (financial, health, or academic) and decides to step in to assist or helps a team member who's having difficulty coming to work due to a transportation problem, for example.

A twenty-year-old college student, Walter Carr, got his first job at a moving company but had difficulty getting to work when his car broke down. Unfortunately, his new job was twenty miles away. He called his friends and girlfriend for a ride, but no one was available to help. Walter "checked his GPS and saw that without a car it would take him 7 hours from his house in Homewood, Alabama, to the town of Pelham for his first day at Bellhops Moving Company" (Yancey-Bragg 2018).

Within a day the story was shared on social media about a thousand times, and when the company's CEO read the story, he was moved to action and not only gifted his car to Walter but set up a GoFundMe campaign and raised $8,500 within twenty-four hours of creating the account. The moral of the story is that compassion work has a ripple effect, and it requires deliberate action to be compassionate.

When we help somebody who is in need and if somebody else hears the news and is compelled to do a good deed for someone else, compassion work has been replicated. It takes one bold, decisive action to provoke another. The application of showing compassion is indiscriminately universal. We might ask, "If compassion work has a ripple effect and requires a deliberate action, why aren't more people practicing compassion?" Compassion is more a natural instinct than a learned behavior; however, ignorance of the benefits of showing compassion could hinder us from practicing it.

It has been proven that relating with others in a meaningful way helps us enjoy better mental and physical health, speeds up recovery from diseases, and may even lengthen our life span (Seppala 2013). The same study showed that in 2012, only 26.5 percent of Americans did volunteer work. Lack of awareness could evidently be the cause of why we are not as compassionate as we could be. I'm certain that if we can intentionally practice compassion at home, in the workplace, and in social gatherings, we can transform our marriages, business relationships, and the quality of our friendships. The understanding that our psychological well-being is enhanced when we give to others who need our assistance is convincingly relevant.

Think about the last time you experienced someone helping an elderly person at the bus stop or protecting a child who was in harm's way. The feeling of doing good for others is much more pleasurable than spending money on ourselves (Seppala 2013). We know this fact to be true: giving makes us happier, a universal feeling irrespective of socioeconomic landscapes or religious affiliation. Living a life of meaning and purpose is also associated with people who focus less on satisfying themselves and more on helping others, which translates into a life rich in compassion, altruism, and greater meaning (Seppala 2013).

An act must have these three elements to be considered compassionate: recognizing suffering, relating to people in their suffering, and reacting to suffering (Sinclair et al. 2017).

Recognizing suffering is important because it will help us behave accordingly without disrespecting the sufferer. Suffering can occur in varied ways, including grieving for our loved ones, struggling with a particular subject (e.g., a math test), going through a divorce, fighting a terminal illness, suffering from loneliness, and enduring a host of other sufferings. So, the ability to recognize and be sensitive to suffering is critical in human relationships and the compassion process. The inability to recognize suffering could affect how we relate with one another.

When we are able to recognize it, we can know how to relate with people in that state. It can be as simple as sitting with them, without pretending to know what they are going through, and giving them moral support or a listening ear when they want to vent or share. Sometimes if we have experienced that state before, we can offer words of encouragement or share our stories in passing, not as the focus of the discussion. The main issue is to be able to relate with them in a nonjudgmental atmosphere, which could lead to extending our hands to help.

When we recognize suffering and relate with people who are suffering, then we can react and help them. This is critical because that's how compassion is demonstrated: by giving support in any way necessary with the sufferer's permission.

Permit me to stop here to allow you to self-reflect on what has been discussed in this chapter. We talked about the golden rule. Compassion is like a mirror that reflects back to us. On *Britain's Got Talent*, Simon gave the contestant radical feedback that propelled him to perform better. We all can relate to Simon and Gruffydd Wyn Roberts's experience, especially when we need encouragement. Walter Carr's first job also depicts human compassion in action; he decided to walk twenty miles to work, which compelled the CEO to gift his car to Walter for his dedication.

We feel better when we engage in giving rather than receiving and are quick to respond to suffering when we can recognize and relate to people who are suffering. On this note, we desire to treat others as we want to be treated.

13

Empowering Cast Members

Lee Cockerell (2018) says it best,

> Be the same person 24 hours a day. Don't change
> when you come to work. Sometimes leaders act
> unnatural at work. Treat everyone with respect.
> Be humble. You are there to help support and
> inspire your team, not to tell them what to do.
> Tell them the outcome you want and they will
> figure out how to deliver the results.

Some decades ago, I had the opportunity to work as a cast member at Disney World, and I learned a great lesson from a colleague about empowering cast members. One day as I and another cast member, Elaine, were preparing to clean a room for a guest, she overheard a little girl talking about how much she loved Tinker Bell. After they left for an errand and we finished cleaning the room, Elaine found a Tinker Bell pin and left it on the little girl's pillow.

When the little girl came back to her room and saw the pin, she was overjoyed with tears. That simple gesture was most remembered by the guest because it was unique and spoke volumes about customer care and compassion.

I also remember this experience because of the impression and message it represents. As simple and insignificant as it may have seemed, the guest at Disney showed more appreciation for it than anything else she received. It took very little time to place the Tinker Bell pin under the guest's pillow, yet it left a long-lasting impression on both the guest and me. It was the least-expected gesture that could possibly affect guests, yet amazingly it became the most talked about event. It is not what we do that matters the most; it is how we do it that speaks volumes.

I'm sure that was not the first time that people making subtle gestures at hotels made an impression on a guest, but the authenticity and simplicity associated with this particular gesture made a world of a difference. The *how* in what we do requires thoughtfulness and deliberate action. After talking with Lee Cockerell, executive vice president of operations for Walt Disney World Resort, about empowering cast members, I further learned how important it is to empower employees in the workplace. I learned that cast members at Disney are empowered to be creative so they are able to demonstrate compassion in real time.

Lee and I said the Tinker Bell pin was a more powerful gesture than if he had given the guests a free room for the night. Generations of family and friends would be passing on that story, all because of a simple gesture from a cast member and an environment that promotes employee empowerment.

One source defines empowerment as a condition whereby employees have the authority to make decisions for taking action in their work area without prior approval (Gulzar et al. 2016). I apply this lesson of empowering team members in our corporation to encourage others in order to continue promoting the lessons of employee empowerment. I'm certain that empowering employees is critical for moving an organization forward in terms of teamwork, deadlines, organizational commitment, management-employee relationships, workplace civility, and so many other positive factors that contribute to organizational success. Empowering employees in the workplace promotes trust, acknowledges employees' competences, and encourages healthy human relationships.

Conversely, I have witnessed situations where employee empowerment was not encouraged. I could feel the tension in the room, especially when projects were approaching deadlines and team members were disengaged without any sense of focus and organization. At that moment, it takes a team member with compassion and emotional stability to bring the team back together, knowing the possible consequences of having a disengaged team. Bringing calmness into a chaotic situation requires a person to be emotionally ready; otherwise it will be necessary for someone to understand the emotional development of self as a prerequisite to giving compassion when needed in an organization (Wei, Zhu, and Li 2016).

It is important for leaders in organizations to create an environment that promotes corporate compassion in the workplace. An environment must encourage team members to look out for one another in stressful situations and to have a sense of "moral self," such as being wise, faithful, thoughtful, and conscientious (Wei, Zhu, and Li 2016). These are some of the effective qualities that could help encourage employee empowerment and compassionate teams, leading to organizational success.

I discovered Dr. Nido R. Qubein and his writings last year when I was researching colleges for my son. The last sentence in the previous paragraph mentioned organizational success to highlight the overarching aim of running a business, but significance tends to be more important than success, according to Qubein.

Qubein suggested that success is secular while significance is spiritual. While I agree with his position that significance is more important than success, in my opinion, success and significance are relevant in their own ways.

Qubein laid more emphasis on significance, although he recognized the importance of entertaining both. You may ask, "How do success and significance relate to employee empowerment?" Everyone wants to be successful in their own ways, as success is both subjective and secular. In other words, we individually define what success means to us.

As a person who practices leadership, I think it is of great importance to create a work environment in which employees define their own success as it relates to organizational tasks—as long as those tasks are well defined and reasonable. For example, tasking a company's sales department to increase sales by ten thousand sales in a week is a projection. It is left to the department head and their crew to strategize how to achieve that goal based on individual team member contributions. Success is focused on tasks, while significance is focused on purpose (Qubein 2012).

When a goal is defined, it is easier to stay on task, and the team members further determines how to achieve such a goal, especially if they are empowered to achieve it in their own ways without violating any corporate policies.

Significance, however, is rooted in purpose. We always ask questions like "Why am I here? Who am I?" and other spiritual questions. How we answer these questions determines how successful we are as a whole in everything we do. In other words, significance relates directly to what we anchor ourselves in, such as faith, family, and friends (Qubein 2012).

Everyone is connected to at least one of these three Fs (faith, family, and friends) as a foundation of social and spiritual existence. I'm convinced that any organization that wants to thrive should ensure that their employees' sense of purpose and meaningfulness is respected and aligned with organizational goals. I must also note that people want to feel significant in a sense of connecting to something outside of themselves, such as, faith, family, and friends (Anderson 2010).

Once we recognize the importance of honoring our employees' sense of significance by empowering them to make decisions that connect to who they are, the chances of achieving organizational success will be much higher. In the final analysis, the extent to which we empower our employees has a direct impact on how they relate to each team member, management, and their environment.

I have observed that empowerment is liberating and inspiring throughout my adult life. The Tinker Bell pin story that I shared is one example. This story proved in a great way the power of employee empowerment and the effect of doing little things.

What made the experience unique was how it was done in terms of the thought process, who was involved—Elaine and I as cast members—and the conversation I had with Lee Cockerell. I also mentioned how Qubein's success and significance assessment can be connected to employee empowerment, because how people view success differs by person. There's no such thing as one definition of success because it's subjective and secular.

Significance or a sense of meaningfulness is another value that employees bring to the workplace. Employees come to work with a sense of significance and meaningfulness; it is up to the organization's leadership to respect team members' values and to ensure they align with the organization's values.

14

I Remembered You

I was simultaneously pleased and humbled after reading an email a staff member sent. She was thanking me for giving a speech at the fall East All Staff meeting over ten years ago. At the meeting's close, I told a story about how important it is to take some time to relax. My staff member's email said she enjoyed the speech but never applied it until she was in a foreign land.

One day she was out and about with a friend, having dinner with light wine. As they finished dinner and were on their way out, it started to rain heavily. For some reason, she decided to run as fast as she could across the street, thinking she would avoid messing her hair up. Lo and behold, as she was halfway across the street, she was soaked. She was mad at herself for not being able to prevent this from happening.

Right in the middle of this episode, she recalled the speech in which I had talked about "letting your hair down and laughing and playing with my children in the rain." Immediately she started laughing and jumping in the rain. My staff member's story was a perfect picture of compassion on display, when someone recalls a pleasant moment that helps ease his or her suffering. Having a positive view of our circumstances changes the outcome.

Her story really made my day. It exemplifies the message I've always talked about, being authentic and vulnerable so people may learn from associating with us. Considering other challenges my staff member was having in the foreign land, such as the language barrier, work in the rain forest, inconsistent power, culture shock, multiple calls to check on family in the United States, bug bites, and overwhelming personal and professional feelings, she remembered a speech I had given that eased her day.

From her description about her trip, the experience was quite different from the life she was used to in the States, but it took one pleasant moment to add a smile to her face. I'm particularly grateful that my words influenced her positively enough to motivate her to pen her experience to me. Even though the speech occurred in a work environment, it still influenced her in her social environment. I'm convinced that just as humanity does not stop existing when we are in the workplace, neither does compassion. As we show compassion to our family members and friends, we should extend it to our work colleagues.

If we can pause and take a self-inventory about how we spend our time at work, we can decide whether we are living life or surviving. There's a difference between living and surviving. Living is when we take time to observe and appreciate everything that comes our way (good or not so good), for lessons and opportunities lie in the midst of our challenges. Living is being human at all times, caring for one another, assisting one another, and enjoying the moment. Living is paying attention in the moment, listening to what nature is telling us—the trees, birds, wind, weather, and silence at night. There's so much to learn if we can just pause for a moment and observe how we inhale oxygen and exhale carbon dioxide. Living is listening to our favorite music and hearing the lyrics and the instruments used to produce the melody. Living is dancing with our loved ones and whispering to them how much they mean to us. Living is giving to the needy; living is being present.

In our quest to live, the universe and energy answer our hearts' desires. I say to you, my friends and relatives, live life, for the next breath is not guaranteed.

On the contrary, surviving life is when we intensely focus our energy on our problems and are barely waiting to make it the next moment, anticipating a subsequent problem to come. Surviving is when we have the "me against the world" mind-set, when we are so involved in our misfortunes that we exaggerate our circumstances to the point of strangling our possibilities. Surviving is constantly worrying about our next bills and debt without doing anything to increase our income or properly managing our finances. Surviving is when we blame others for our hardships in life instead of developing a solution-driven mind-set.

There's so much in life besides paying bills and worrying ourselves to death. The choice is up to us to remember those moments that made a difference in our lives.

There is power in remembering. Whether good or not so good, experiences have lessons to teach us. If we choose to remember the good experiences, it does something to our psychological well-being, and our brains will help us to remember more good moments. I'm certain that if we really want to remember good moments, we can find plenty of them because they are all around us. In just twenty-four hours, we can find something that will make us remember good or not-so-good moments, but we have to pay attention in order to recognize them. By paying attention, we come to appreciate our time and moments with people. Remembering the moments is critical because both types of moments have lessons to teach us. Good moments teach us to be grateful, and gratitude is a medicine to the body.

Gratitude has the healing power to turn things around for us, simply because we view our circumstances through the lens of gratitude. Conversely, challenges expose us to new possibilities. Growth, whether financial, relational, social, or spiritual, emerges from difficult experiences. But if we can view those bumpy moments as learning curves, we can gain a wealth of knowledge from them. Challenges teach us how to be either humble or arrogant, depending on how we perceive them.

Let's think about challenges this way for a moment. If there's no resistance, a ship cannot sail on the sea. There's no victory without a fight. A plant can't grow without breaking the ground to come up to the surface, and the list goes on.

Challenges are catalysts for change. The way we perceive change determines the type of change we will encounter. It is up to us to remember which approach worked for us previously and which one didn't. When we self-reflect, we can point out those moments that worked for us. All we have to do is to remember them.

I recall those days when we wanted to relocate to North Carolina from New York. It was never a fear-free moment, but we did it. And when it was time to move to Arizona from North Carolina, it was never easy, but we also did it. None of those moves came without stress and new challenges, but we did them anyway because we had an agenda. I've yet to see any successful person who has never feared the unknown, yet they did it anyway. Whatever we are looking for is on the other side of our fears. If we can turn our destructive fears into constructive ones, we will, for once, have a new experience (Agbanyim 2013).

Remembering the moments is always therapeutic,

depending on what we intend to do with the information. Even remembering not-so-good moments teaches us what not to repeat. That alone is a lesson in itself. So however, we look at recalling the moments, there's always something to learn from them because it puts our emotions on trial. All the feelings we thought we had buried pop up to the surface as a yardstick to measure how well we have dealt with that particular event. Allow every circumstance and memory to be a teaching moment and a case in point, for with this mind-set comes new lessons and memories.

Thank you very much for reading this heartfelt chapter. I wrote it out of gratitude. To be remembered in such a positive light brings fulfilment into my life. I say this with absolute humility because I was not expecting to receive the reward from my work in real time. I do believe that what we do at work has a ripple effect outside of work and vice versa.

"I Remembered You" is everyone's story. It's a tale everyone wishes to hear at least once in a lifetime. Whether we remembered what someone did to us that wasn't so good or was great, there's always a lesson to be learned from it only if we can look beyond the obvious hurt and suffering.

As we know, human suffering is inevitable, and we should acknowledge it without shame so we can find positive ways to turn our pains into promises and possibilities. Suffering is necessary for growth, for without suffering, there will be no growth. Without resistance, a ship cannot sail in the high sea.

Imagine if the ship builders were afraid of the resistance before they started building ships. They would have been no ships today. But in spite of their fears, they forged ahead and built ships. So I'm convinced that whatever we are looking for is on the other side of our fears. Build it anyway and see what possibilities we can bring to our hurting world.

Afterword

*T*here is power in storytelling. Most lessons I have learned through these many years were derived from shared stories. I now realize that human connections are more impactful when we share our stories, whether they are painful or happy in nature. I have also learned how to be compassionate, accepting, forgiving, and vulnerable by engaging with people, either through their stories or my own. I am convinced that if we can tell our stories more often to both familiar and unfamiliar faces, we will start to realize that emotions carry universal meanings.

Love has no color. Forgiveness has no gender. Compassion has no age limit. The power to accept others is available to each and every one of us, as is our mutual vulnerability, which serves as a gateway to our humanity.

I'm convinced that if we allow ourselves to be open to new possibilities through storytelling, those things that used to bother us will start to teach us lessons that we never knew existed. I'm a living testament to the reality that my work in the area of vulnerability has changed my life beyond measure. That work continues to this day. I invite you to take a look at old stories through a new lens, because I did (and still do) and it has changed my life for the better. I look forward to learning from everyone's stories as well as my own.

Index

References

Aboul-Ela, Ghadeer Mohamed Badr ElDin. 2017. "Reflections on Workplace Compassion and Job Performance." *Journal of Human Values* 23 (3): 234–243. doi:10.1177/0971685817713285.

Agbanyim, J. I. 2013. *Fear: A Healthy Emotion If Well Managed.* Bloomington, IN: iUniverse.

Alexander, E. 2012. *Proof of Heaven: A Neurosurgeon's Journey into Afterlife.* New York: Simon & Schuster.

Anderson, M. 2010. "Significance: Teaching with a Sense of Purpose." In *The Well-Balanced Teacher: How to Work Smarter and Stay Sane Inside the Classroom and Out*, 47–64. Alexandria, VA: ASCD.

Andrews, E. "Did a Premature Obituary Inspire the Nobel Prize?" https://www.history.com/news/did-a-premature-obituary-inspire-the-nobel-prize.

Bassett, R. L. 2006. "Forgiveness Is a Choice." *Journal of Psychology and Christianity* 25(4): 358.

"Be a Keeper." http://www.cathappy.net/keepers.htm.

Brown, B. "The Power of Vulnerability." https://www.youtube.com/watch?v=iCvmsMzlF7o.

Cockerell, L. "Leadership Thoughts." https://www.leecockerell.com/.

Cuddy, A. "TEDTalk: Your Body Language May Shape Who You Are." https://www.youtube.com/watch?v=Ks-_Mh1QhMc.

David, S. "The Gift and Power of Emotional Courage." https://www.youtube.com/watch?v=NDQ1Mi5I4rg

Goldman, A. 2008. "Leadership Negligence and Malpractice: Emotional Toxicity at SkyWaves Aerospace International." Emerald Group Publishing Limited. doi:10.1016/S1746-9791(08)04009-1.

"Nervous Welsh Opera Singer Gets Golden Buzzer from Amanda Holden on *Britain's Got Talent*." https://www.youtube.com/watch?v=ggZ0kjYqC34.

Gulzar, S. A., R. Karmaliani, S. S. Noorani, and A. A. Shah. 2016. "Empowerment among Women Nurses: A Conceptual Review of Literature." *I-Manager's Journal on Nursing* 6 (4): 20.

Harris, M. "2002 Interview: Reginald Denny Looks Back on the LA Riots, Get-Well Cards." https://www.nbclosangeles.com/news/local/Reginald-Denny-Looks-Back-on-the-LA-Riots--149165165.html.

Hicks, V. J. 2018. "A Dose of Forgiveness." *Obstetrics & Gynecology* 132 (4): 811–812. doi:10.1097/AOG.0000000000002909.

Hinds, J. "Motivational Stories: The Life We Choose." http://www.getmotivation.com/stories8.htm.

"History of the City." http://www.rensselaerny.gov/AboutCity.aspx.

Kevin. "No Handshake for You." https://www.youtube.com/watch?v=ovo7uA8JrCk.

Marcom Web Group. "Claim: The Unexamined Life Is Not Worth Living." https://www.plu.edu/marcom/news/2010/04/19/claim-the-unexamined-life-is-not-worth-living.

Merriam-Webster. "Compassion." https://www.merriam-webster.com/dictionary/compassion.

Navarro, J. 2018. *The Dictionary of Body Language: A Field-Guide to Human Behavior.* New York: William Marrow Publishing.

Qubein, N. R. "An Excerpt from Seven Choices for Success and Significance." http://www.pokerheadrush.com/2012/08/27/an-excerpt-from-seven-choices-for-success-and-significance-by-dr-nido-r-qubein.

Raj, M., and S. S. Wiltermuth. 2016. "Barriers to Forgiveness." *Social and Personality Psychology Compass* 10 (11): 679–690. doi:10.1111/spc3.12290.

Rensselaer, New York. "Population in 2014." http://www.city-data.com/city/Rensselaer-New-York.html.

Rhodes, K. "A Mind that Is Stretched by a New Experience Can Never Go Back to Its Old Dimensions." https://medium.com/havas-lofts/well-said-oliver-wendell-holmes-jr-american-lawyer-and-this-week-s-inspiration-85f49a98234a.

Riley, N. S. "The Parents Who Didn't Sue Disney Taught America a Powerful Lesson." https://nypost.com/2016/07/23/the-parents-who-didnt-sue-disney-taught-america-a-powerful-lesson.

Rivera, D. "The Power to Define Reality: Whose Reality Is Real?" https://www.psychologytoday.com/us/blog/microaggressions-in-everyday-life/201010/the-power-define-reality.

Scott. K. 2017. *Radical Candor: Be a Kick-Ass Boss without Losing Your Humanity.* New York: St. Martin's Press.

Seppala, E. "The Compassionate Mind." https://www.psychologicalscience.org/observer/the-compassionate-mind.

Shapiro, B. 2011. "Let Go of the Past: The Benefits of Forgiveness." *Washington Jewish Week*, September 22, 2011. https://search-proquest-com.contentproxy.phoenix.edu/docview/903304314?accountid=35812.

Sinclair, S., K. Beamer, T. F. Hack, S. McClement, S. Raffin Bouchal, H. M. Chochinov, and N. A. Hagen. 2017. "Sympathy, Empathy, and Compassion: A Grounded Theory Study of Palliative Care Patients' Understandings, Experiences, and Preferences." *Palliative Medicine* 31 (5): 437–447. doi:10.1177/0269216316663499.

Southwick, S. M. and D. S. Charney. 2012. *Resilience: The Science of Mastering Life's Greatest Challenges.* Cambridge: Cambridge University Press.

Swindoll, R. C. "Charles R. Swindoll Quotes." https://www.goodreads.com/author/quotes/5139.Charles_R_Swindoll.

Szalavitz, M., and B. Perry. 2011. *Born for Love: Why Empathy Is Essential—and Endangered.* New York: HarperCollins Publishers.

The Nobel Prize. "Alfred Nobel's Life and Work." https://www.nobelprize.org/alfred-nobel/alfred-nobels-life-and-work.

"UPS Retires 'What Can Brown Do for You' Slogan." https://dailycaller.com/2010/09/13/ups-retires-what-can-brown-do-for-you-slogan.

Wei, H., Y. Zhu, and S. Li. 2016. "Top Executive Leaders' Compassionate Actions: An Integrative Framework of Compassion Incorporating a Confucian Perspective." *Asia Pacific Journal of Management* 33 (3): 767–787. doi:10.1007/s10490-016-9463-2.

White, J. A. 1998. "Leadership through Compassion and Understanding." *Journal of Management Inquiry* 7 (4): 286.

Williamson, M. 1996. *A Return to Love: Reflections on the Principles of A Course in Miracles.* New York: HarperOne Publisher.

Wilson, T., A. Milosevic, M. Carroll, K. Hart, and S. Hibbard. 2008. "Physical Health Status in Relation to Self-Forgiveness and Other-Forgiveness in Healthy College Students." *Journal of Health Psychology* 13 (6): 798–803. doi:10.1177/1359105308093863.

Wright, K. "Dare to Be Yourself. Being True to Oneself Is Not for the Faint of Heart." https://www.psychologytoday.com/us/articles/200805/dare-be-yourself.

Yancey-Bragg, N. "Alabama College Student Walks almost 20 Miles Overnight to First Day of Work; CEO Gives Him His Car." https://www.usatoday.com/story/news/nation-now/2018/07/17/alabama-man-walks-14-miles-work-ceo-gifts-him-car/792519002/.

About the Authors

Robert Ackerman earned his bachelor's degree from the college of Saint Rose and has held several positions within the New York state government. He currently serves as the senior vice president and chief operating officer of a wireless infrastructure company. He is married and has five children.

J. Ibeh Agbanyim is a Harvard Kennedy School¬–trained leadership development practitioner, best-selling author, public speaker, and organizational psychology consultant. The founder of Focused Vision Consulting, LLC, he has been a senior logistics associate at UPS for over twenty-two years. He holds a graduate degree in industrial-organizational psychology.

www.ingramcontent.com/pod-product-compliance
Lightning Source LLC
Chambersburg PA
CBHW050359290526
45786CB00003B/1054